T0339972

"Having been in franchising for over 30 years, I have seen the franchise business model enable countless people get into business for themselves but not by themselves. This textbook is an excellent deep dive into franchising and will bring knowledge and value to students, others wanting to learn about franchising, and those who are considering becoming a franchisor or franchisee."

—**Catherine Monson**, *President of Propelled Brands, Past President of the International Franchise Association*

"Ed Teixeira and Richard Chan's book on franchising is a gateway to an expansive professional career. As a franchisee, franchisor, franchise company board member, professor teaching franchising and having written my dissertation on franchising, I say, hallelujah! Indeed, I believe franchising is the business genesis of economic networking.This book provides the underpinning of knowledge commensurate with a concentrated MBA. You will discover a wide spectrum of entrepreneurial opportunities in franchising."

—**Steve Stephen Spinelli Jr, PhD**, *President, Babson College*

"This book is a must for prospective and current franchisees who want to understand all facets of the franchise business model. The authors convey their deep expertise in a highly readable way. They cover the gamut from understanding the key elements and value of the franchise model, including its evolution, to its continued promise for today and the future. Franchisees will refer to the book often as a guide to all the key elements of a franchise including intellectual property, financing, marketing, operations, and human resources."

—**Manuel London, PhD**, *Dean, College of Business, SUNY Distinguished Professor, State University of New York at Stony Brook*

Franchising Strategies

A comprehensive and accessible companion to a proven business model, this book shows how to franchise an existing business, supported by case studies, data, and research reports on the franchise industry.

From small- to medium-sized businesses, franchising can lead to successful and profitable growth, and plays an important role within the U.S. economy. Utilizing a proprietary dataset with the most up-to-date statistics regarding a range of franchising trends, this analytical guide is based on management research frameworks that will lead to better understanding of a range of franchising strategies. Issues covered include the following:

- The franchising business model, including its history, economic impact, and regulations.
- Critical factors that significantly influence franchising success, enabling a comprehensive feasibility analysis of franchising potential or existing business ideas.
- Implementation components of franchising strategies, such as different franchise structures, regional development plans, and future trends.

With its clear focus and practical orientation, this book will be a valuable resource for entrepreneurs, as well as undergraduate and postgraduate students, interested in acquiring the knowledge, skills, and abilities to succeed in franchising.

Ed Teixeira is the VP of Franchise Development for FranchiseGrade.com and has 40 years of experience in the franchise industry including the retail, manufacturing, home health care, and medical staffing industries. He has done franchising in Asia, Europe, and South America. Ed has a Master's in Economics, Northeastern University. He is a member of the Advisory Board at Pace University Lubin School of Business and Industry Partner with Stony Brook University.

Richard Chan is an Associate Professor in the College of Business and has founded the Center of Entrepreneurial Finance at Stony Brook University, U.S.A. His research situates at the intersection of technology and entrepreneurship. Specifically, he investigates how entrepreneurs finance their ventures using emerging platforms, such as crowdfunding and blockchain-based cryptocurrency. His work has appeared in leading entrepreneurship journals.

Franchising Strategies

The Entrepreneur's Guide to Success

Ed Teixeira and Richard Chan

Routledge
Taylor & Francis Group

NEW YORK AND LONDON

Cover image: © Parradee Kietsirikul

First published 2023
by Routledge
605 Third Avenue, New York, NY 10158

and by Routledge
4 Park Square, Milton Park, Abingdon, Oxon, OX14 4RN

Routledge is an imprint of the Taylor & Francis Group, an informa business

Library of Congress Cataloguing-in-Publication Data
Names: Teixeira, Ed, author. | Chan, Richard (Professor of Business)
author.
Title: Franchising strategies : the entrepreneur's guide to success / Ed
Teixeira and Richard Chan.
Description: New York, NY : Routledge, 2022. | Includes
bibliographical references and index. |
Identifiers: LCCN 2021061730 | ISBN 9780367472351 (hardback) |
ISBN 9780367458423 (paperback) | ISBN 9781003034285 (ebook)
Subjects: LCSH: Franchises (Retail trade) | Small business--
Management. | Strategic planning.
Classification: LCC HF5429.23 .T45 2022 | DDC 658.8/708--dc23/eng/
20211220
LC record available at https://lccn.loc.gov/2021061730

ISBN: 978-0-367-47235-1 (hbk)
ISBN: 978-0-367-45842-3 (pbk)
ISBN: 978-1-003-03428-5 (ebk)

DOI: 10.4324/9781003034285

Typeset in Sabon
by MPS Limited, Dehradun

To my wife Carol who has provided encouragement, inspiration, and support throughout my entire business career and during the writing of this book and to my son Eddie and daughter Denise who provided me with her Word skills. To Richard my coauthor, who helped me to apply my business knowledge to educate students and future entrepreneurs. Also, to the countless franchisees, franchisors, and professionals who have striven and continue to strive to uphold and adhere to ethical standards of franchising.

—Ed Teixeira

To my parents C.H. and M.J., and my brothers Eric and Victor who have provided a nurturing environment that made me who I am. To my wife Amanda and my children Alexis, Terence, and Leo who have encouraged me to be who I could be. To my coauthor Ed who have generously shared his insights and experiences and patiently gone through the long writing process. To generations of courageous entrepreneurs, who have inspired me to tackle the financing piece of the startup puzzle.

— Richard Chan

Contents

Acknowledgments

The authors gratefully acknowledge the contributions made by the following individuals to the content and information in this book.

Individual Contributors

Alicia Miller, Co-Founder and Managing Director of Catalyst Insight Group

Barry Knepper, The Franchise CPA

Carl Zwisler, Senior Counsel at Lathrop GPM LLP

Colin Gaffney, President and COO, Fran Start, LLC

Craig Slavin, Author, Speaker, Certified Navigator Coach, Values-based Advisor

Craig Tractenberg, Co-Chair-Franchise and Distribution Practice and Co-Chair International Arbitration Practice at Fox Rothschild LLP

Doug Kushell, President Franchise Search, Inc.

Eddy Goldberg, Managing Editor at Franchise Update Media

Eleanor Vaida Gerhards, National Co-Chair of Franchising and Distribution Group Fox Rothchild, LLP

Elizabeth Dillon, Chair of Franchise & Distribution Group at Lathrop GPM

Eric Stites, CEO and Managing Director, Franchise Business Review

Gary Occhiogrosso, Managing Partner at Franchise Growth Solutions

Harold Kestenbaum, President at HLK P.C. Law Firm Partner at Spadea Lignana

Jeff Bevis, Servant Leader | Business Builder | Franchising Expertise | Post-Acute Care Visionary | Domestic and International | Forbes Contributor

Jeff Lefler, CEO at Franchise Grade

Jeffrey Goldstein, Nationally Recognized Franchise Lawyer & Antitrust Attorney

Jimma Bennett, Uni Shippers
John Cunningham, Founder and CEO Vehicle Tracking Solutions
John Gordon, Principal at Pacific Management Consulting Group
Julie Lusthaus, Franchise & Business Attorney Lusthaus Law P.C.
Keith Gerson, President of Franchise Operations for FranConnect
Mark Jameson, Chief Propelled Brands
Mary Ann O'Connell Franwise
Michael Einbinder, Einbinder & Dunn LLP
Michael Moccia, Graphic Designs, Inc.
Mitch Cohen, Franchisee at Sola Salon Studios and Jersey Mike's
Mitch Pickney, The Franchise Consultant Company
Paul Pickett, Chief Development Officer at Wild Birds Unlimited, Inc.
Paulo Mauro, President Global Franchise Network
Richard Rosen, Richard L. Rosen Law Firm. NYC, NY
Steve Begelman, Founder SMB Franchise Advisors
Tom Spadea, Spadea Lignana Franchise Attorneys

Chapter 1

Introduction to Franchising

From small- to medium-sized businesses, franchising has evolved into a proven business model that can lead to successful and profitable growth. An economic forecast conducted by FRANdata for the International Franchise Association (IFA) in February of 2021 projects that franchising's contribution to the U.S. economy is forecast to grow by 7% in 2021. More than 26,000 new franchised businesses will open in 2021, recovering most of the losses felt in the previous year due to COVID-19. Franchises will employ some 8.3 million people, adding nearly 800,000 new jobs.[1] Much of this employment will be in the retail, food, and services industries. Franchising creates many jobs, and some will be entry-level jobs for lower-skilled workers. Franchising offers these entry-level workers skills and job training and helps them to develop, leading to career advancement. The growth of franchise businesses is robust, making franchising an important economic development strategy on the national level.

The franchise business model plays an important role within the U.S. economy. In 2019, the economic output of franchise establishments in the United States was about $787.5 billion and represented 3% of the country's GDP. In a 2021 report called The Value of Franchising, Oxford Economics found that franchise businesses provide better pay and benefits than nonfranchised businesses, are diverse in industry and ownership, and offer entrepreneurial opportunities especially to women, people of color, and veterans. The report found that franchise businesses drive 1.8 times higher sales than comparable nonfranchise establishments, provide 2.3 times as many jobs than their nonfranchise counterparts, and provide a path to entrepreneurship that one-third of franchisees reported was critical to their chance to own a business at all.[2]

The complexity and potential benefits of franchising highlight the importance of understanding how it works. Although scholars have studied franchising along with its antecedents and consequences for over five decades,[3] their findings have circulated mostly among academics and are generally not available to those entrepreneurs who might benefit

DOI: 10.4324/9781003034285-1

from such knowledge, a finding that prompted us to organize and present the information contained in this book.

In this chapter, we define what franchising is and what it is not and go on to discuss the major theoretical frameworks in management research that are relevant to understanding franchising strategies. We illustrate franchising history by describing how the franchise industry has evolved and grown into a dynamic business model exported throughout the world. We also highlight its corresponding advantages and disadvantages. We conclude by presenting the economic impact of franchising, the various franchise sectors and categories, and relevant data pertaining to these franchises.

Definition of Franchising

Franchising is a business model that comprises contractual agreements between two groups of entrepreneurs: a franchisor who created a venture to advance an entrepreneurial opportunity, and a group of franchisees who purchase the right to use the brand name, operating process, and marketing system of that venture in new geographic markets.[4] In such a relationship, the franchisor not only grants a license to a third party in order to conduct business under their trademark, and specify the products and services to be offered by franchisees, but provide them with an operating system, brand, training, and marketing and logistic support.

Although franchising often involves the use of a license, it is distinct from licensing, another entrepreneurial growth strategy. Licensing refers to an agreement whereby a company (the licenser) grants the right to utilize intangible assets as a brand, such as intellectual property or an operation process, in exchange for buying and selling the company's products or services. Franchising is more than just the use of licensing, however: it is a contractual arrangement in which the franchisor allows the franchisee to conduct business using the brand or intellectual property as an independently operated entity within its franchise network. Licensees usually make a significant capital investment in designing and implementing their business operations. They may receive operational and marketing support from the franchisor in exchange for royalty fees. Table 1.1 below summarizes the comparison between franchising and licensing.

Major Theoretical Frameworks

Scholars have utilized several theoretical frameworks to explain the nature, antecedents, and consequences of franchising strategies. Two main examples are resource scarcity and agency theory.[5] Early researchers proposed resource scarcity to explain why firms would exchange firm ownership with financial capital to grow their business and increase

Table 1.1 Franchising versus Licensing

	Franchising	Licensing
Trademark and Branding	Uses a common trademark or brand which can develop strong brand recognition.	They are identified by the business name of the Licensee. Challenging to promote strong branding.
Support	Franchisors supply trademarks, training, marketing, and ongoing support.	Minimal or no training, typically no ongoing support.
Standards	Franchisors require franchisees to meet performance standards and adhere to operational guidelines.	Limited guidelines that licensee must follow.
Noncompete	Franchise agreements have strong in-term and post-term noncompete provisions.	Little or no noncompete provisions.
Start-Up Costs	May be more costly to startup and run.	Usually less costly to start and operate.
Fees	Franchisees pay initial fees and royalty fees based on revenues.	Most licensing agreements do not have an initial startup, royalty, or continuing fees. There may be product purchase expenses.
Network Growth	A stronger brand image through the franchise model and familiar brand name.	As licensees use their company names, lack of typical brand name, which may diminish brand recognition.

market shares. However, this framework fell out of favor when increasing studies illustrated the lack of empirical support for the resource scarcity perspective.[6] Indeed, firms do not need to limit ownership for business growth to result from franchising, as there are alternative funding sources that could be less costly and more efficiently acquired.

Eventually, agency theory became the dominant framework that explains the usage of franchising strategy. It was originally developed to explain the interplay between two stakeholders, the principal and the agent. In a typical setup, the agent makes decisions on behalf of the principal, but such decisions may favor the interests of the agent rather than the principal. Franchising provides a powerful incentive to align the interests of the principal (franchisor) and the agent (franchisee). It can ensure that franchisees invest their own resources to build and operate outlets, reducing the need to monitor franchisees' efforts.[7]

This cost-reduction advantage of franchising strategy does not fully limit the incentives for franchisees which might damage a brand's reputation, keeping many firms small or growing mainly through company ownership. This point recently prompted researchers to advocate for a symbiotic perspective,[8] suggesting that many franchisors adopt a "plural form" of ownership strategy. This strategy describes how many franchisors not only delegate authority to franchisees but also maintain ownership of their own outlets to deter free-riding by franchisees and foster system standardization to protect the franchise's reputation. Recent research has applied other frameworks, such as relational contracts literature and franchise performance data, in order to explain franchising.[9] Such frameworks and related findings will be discussed throughout this book when relevant.

History of Franchising

While the word franchise is derived from the old French, meaning "privilege" or "freedom," franchising is not a new or recent concept; its origins can be traced back thousands of years across different continents. For example, in the Zhou (Chou) dynasty, the kings set up the Feng-Jiang system, giving large domains of land to warriors and relatives in exchange for homage and resources.[10] Similar practices occurred during the Middle Ages in Europe, where kings and lords granted specific individuals (fiefdoms) the right to hunt or conduct business on their lands.[11] Just like today's franchises, these landowners set up mutual agreements with tax collectors who would keep a percentage in exchange for their services.

Franchising became a formal business model in the United States around the 19th century. The Singer Company was the first occurrence of franchising in the United States when it used franchising to distribute its sewing machines.[12] Although the machines sold well, Singer did not earn enough because its dealers had exclusive rights to their territories, which took most of the profits from the franchise operation.

The more traditional form of franchising began in the 1920s when industry trailblazers such as A&W Root Beer and Howard Johnson appeared on the scene. A&W remains in business today while Howard Johnson operates a chain of hotels and motels. Both companies implemented franchise models that seemed simple but had fundamental components that included an initial franchise fee, royalty fees, a standard location design, and similar products. Thus began the structural form of franchising that's evolved into today's franchise companies.

In the 1950s and 1960s, the popularity of franchising ballooned, due in part to the expansion of the U.S. economy and the growth of the interstate highway system. Notable franchises that emerged during this period included familiar brands such as Holiday Inn, Dunkin' Donuts, McDonald's, Burger King, Midas Muffler, 7-Eleven, Wendy's, Dairy Queen, Tastee Freeze, and Sheraton hotels. From 1966 to 1969, approximately 100,000 new franchises commenced operations. These newly emerged franchises were often in the quick-serve and hospitality sectors, based on their ability to package business operations and branding into systems that could be duplicated in multiple locations.

The evolution of the McDonald's and Kentucky Fried Chicken franchises are the most iconic stories in the growth of franchising. Ray Kroc was a salesman for Hamilton Beach appliances. In 1954, when he learned that a restaurant had purchased eight multi-Mixers, he decided to visit the McDonald brothers' hamburger stand in San Bernardino, California. Kroc was so impressed with the McDonald's operation, its cleanliness and the process for preparing and serving food, he believed that the restaurant model could be replicated throughout the United States. The first franchise was opened in Des Plaines, Illinois, in 1955, and eventually led to 36,000 locations worldwide. Kroc's vision for McDonald's grew into reality. To this day, people who visit a McDonald's anywhere in the world expect quality food, cleanliness, and excellent service. No franchise has epitomized the principles of franchising quite like McDonald's.[13]

Founded by Colonel Harland Sanders, Kentucky Fried Chicken began as a roadside restaurant in Corbin, Kentucky. The first franchise opened in 1952 in Utah. KFC became the pioneer of serving chicken in the fast-food industry, with Colonel Sanders a larger-than-life figure in television commercials. The Colonel Sanders image is still prevalent in KFC advertising, especially on television. In 1964, as KFC continued its growth, the Colonel decided to sell to a group of investors led by John Y. Brown and Jack C. Massey. Beginning in the 1960s, KFC was one of the first U.S. fast-food franchises to expand to other countries, opening restaurants in England, Canada, and Mexico. Today KFC has 19,000 locations worldwide. The story of McDonald's and KFC has become synonymous with the history and growth of franchising.[14]

As we enter the 21st century, the franchising model continues to be an essential growth strategy for entrepreneurs. The diffusion of the franchising business model has spread across a variety of industries. According to a recent study, 72% of emerging franchise systems cover a wide range of industries, including personal services, quick-service restaurants, commercial and residential real estate, along with automotive, and retail food.[15] The franchising business model has proven to be resilient. Even in a challenging economic climate, franchise outlets continue to grow.[16]

Over the past few years, multi-unit franchisee companies owned and operated by a parent company have become large enough to become publicly traded companies. Publicly traded mega-franchise companies have the advantage of achieving economies of scale when negotiating with suppliers and other vendors. In addition, they can expand their holdings by acquiring additional franchise rights or other multi-unit franchisee brands. For franchisors, a publicly traded multi-unit franchisee company can provide rapid growth, stability, and high-level management expertise for new units.

The following list of publicly traded franchises is more substantial than most would expect of franchisee owned franchises.

- Carrols Restaurant Group trades on NASDAQ. It owns and operates approximately 675 Burger King franchises. Burger King, the franchisor, has an ownership interest of about 28% in the company.
- Diversified Restaurant Holdings is a NASDAQ company. It owns and operates Buffalo Wild Wings franchises as well as the Bagger Dave's Burger Tavern restaurants.
- Arcos Dorados Holdings trades on the NYSE. It is an Argentinian company that owns and operates more than 1,800 McDonald's restaurants in 20 Latin American countries.
- Meritage Hospitality Group trades over the counter. It owns and operates more than 120 Wendy's and Twisted Rooster restaurants.
- HMS Host operates franchises and affiliate-owned brands in airports and highway rest stops. It is owned by Autogril SpA, a public company in Italy with worldwide operations.

In recent years, private equity firms have become more active investors and majority owners in franchise companies. Private equity (PE) investment can provide the capital needed to grow a franchise system faster than either multi-unit franchisees or franchisors. A PE firm can add earnings to its portfolio by investing in franchise brands that have stability and steady revenue and earnings flow. Private equity firms desire earnings because they are obligated to provide acceptable financial returns to their investors. Their primary goal is a return on investment that will surpass the stock market. Because of their desire for earnings, PE firms can receive negative feedback from unit franchisees who fear that a PE firm will reduce franchise services to increase overall earnings.

PE firms also have multi-unit franchisee holdings:

- Roark Capital Group is one of the largest PE firms that specialize in the franchise industry. Its $19 billion assets under management include large franchise brands that include Anytime Fitness, CKE Restaurants (Carl's Jr., Hardee's, Green Burrito & Red Burritos), Culver's (minority investment), Maaco and Meineke.

- Sun Capital, which owns Heartland Automotive Services, the largest Jiffy Lube franchisee.
- Sentinel Capital owns Border Foods, a Taco Bell franchisee, Sterling Investment Partners owns Southern California Pizza Company, a Pizza Hut franchisee with more than 220 locations.
- NPC International operates more than 1,250 Pizza Hut franchises and 140 Wendy's franchises. NPC was acquired by an entity controlled by Olympus Growth Fund V, LP and certain affiliates in December 2011. At the time of the acquisition, NPC obtained debt financing.
- Morgan's Foods, Inc., the owner of 68 KFC, Taco Bell, and Pizza Hut Express franchises, was a public company until it was acquired in May 2014 by Apex Restaurant Management for roughly $20 million. Apex is one of the largest franchisees of Yum! Brands (KFC, Pizza Hut, and Taco Bell) and Long John Silver restaurants.
- Falcon Holdings LLC operates approximately 100 Church's Chicken restaurants.[17]

As PE and publicly held franchisee entities grow, their access to capital and marketing power enables them to be formidable competitors for unit and multi-unit franchisees. Despite these systemic changes in the franchise industry, the individual or unit franchisee remains the dominant player in franchise operations.

Franchising Regulations and Associations

The rapid growth of franchises in the 1950s led to some instances of franchise abuse and ultimately regulation of the franchise industry, including franchise fairness provisions in federal legislation. In 1956 the federal government established the Automobile Dealer Franchise Act and in 1968 the Federal Petroleum Marketing Practice Act. Both statutes led to the implementation of freestanding franchise legislation in federal and state laws. In the 1970s, many states enacted franchise relationship laws to prevent franchisor abuses such as encroachment, renewal of franchise agreements, discrimination, and wrongful termination of a franchise.

In 1978, the Federal Trade Commission (FTC) enacted the FTC Franchise Rule requiring every franchise to disclose specific information about its business operation model. This information consisted of 23 items, including the history of the franchise, business experience of franchise leadership, franchise litigation, estimated franchise investment, and obligations of the franchisor and franchisee. Because of its importance, this FTC Rule has been amended several times to address emerging issues and clarify specific provisions such as the difference between a protected and exclusive franchise territory and requiring franchisors to show expense data to prospective franchisees.[18]

In addition to the FTC, 15 states (known as the Registration States) have pre-franchise disclosure laws that regulate the offer and sale of a franchise: California, Hawaii, Illinois, Indiana, Maryland, Michigan, Minnesota, New York, North Dakota, Oregon, Rhode Island, South Dakota, Virginia, Washington, and Wisconsin. Such state regulations require the same disclosure as the FTC Rule, utilizing the Franchise Disclosure Document (FDD) format and items. There may be slight differences among the Registration States regarding franchise default and termination notification and noncompete limitations, which reflect individual state statutes and business practices. Ten states require a franchisor to file its FDD with the state before offering a franchise. A filing is a more straightforward process compared with registering an FDD with a Registration State. Those states with a filing requirement usually have regulations covering various business opportunities. These are Connecticut, Florida, Kentucky, Maine, Nebraska, North Carolina, South Carolina, South Dakota, Texas, and Utah.

In addition to federal and state regulations, two franchise trade associations monitor and prevent fraudulent franchising activities in the United States, representing the perspective of franchisors or franchisees:

In 1960, the IFA was founded by a group of franchisors. Its objective was to remove fraudulent franchisors from the industry and reduce unsavory sales practices by salespeople. The founder of Dunkin' Donuts, William Rosenberg, was the leading force behind the formation of the IFA. Today the IFA's mission is to protect, promote, and enhance franchising. It has a strict code of standards for members and serves as an advocate for the growth of the franchise industry and lobbies on behalf of the franchise industry, representing franchisors, franchisees, and suppliers to franchising. It educates prospective franchisees and publishes research articles on franchising. The IFA reports 1,100 franchisor members, 20,000 franchisee members, and 600 supplier members.[19]

The Coalition of Franchisee Associates (CFA) founded in 2007 is comprised of franchisee association leaders dedicated to the development and growth of their own organizations. The CFA provides a forum for its members to share best practices, knowledge, and resources for the benefit of the entire franchisee population. The CFA's mission is to leverage the collective strengths of franchisee associations for the benefit of the franchisee community through involvement in government advocacy via representation on Capitol Hill, key legislation monitoring, participation in grassroots campaigns, CFA Political Action Committee, and access to the CFA legislative web site. The CFA brings together some of the largest and most reputable independent franchisee associations.[20]

International Franchising

Many franchise companies in the United States have expanded to other countries. Successful franchisors generally receive inquiries from international prospects. An IFA survey conducted in 2015 found that 74% of their members wanted to start or accelerate global operations, and 72% believed that worldwide growth would be significant for future success.[21] International expansion has become quite prevalent, with many of the largest franchise systems expanding to more international locations than U.S. locations. Table 1.2 lists the fifteen largest U.S.-owned international brands.

In addition to traditional franchise countries such as France, Japan, Australia, Germany, and the United Kingdom, such countries as Brazil, China, and Mexico have achieved extraordinary growth in franchise systems, importing and launching U.S. franchise brands. An example of how franchising has expanded wide is the 7-Eleven chain of convenience stores, which operates over 68,000 franchises and company stores worldwide. The company is majority-owned by a Japanese company, Seven & I Holdings Co., Ltd., which acquired ownership from its U.S. founders in 1991.

International Franchise Association, members view overseas expansion as a vehicle for growing and diversifying franchise portfolios. A survey of IFA members showed that 61% of respondents currently franchised or operated in international locations, and 16% generated

Table 1.2 List of the 15 Largest U.S. International Brands[a]

Rank	Franchise Company	System Sales (in 1000s)	U.S. Locations	Total Locations
1	McDonald's	$90,910,000	14,029	37,421
2	7-Eleven	$85,000,000	8,357	64,600
3	KFC	$24,515,000	4,109	21,487
4	Burger King	$20,075,100	7,226	16,767
5	Subway	$17,300,000	25,908	43,912
6	Ace Hardware	$15,989,000	4,526	5,229
7	Domino's	$12,252,100	5,587	14,856
8	Pizza Hut	$12,034,000	7,497	16,748
9	Marriott	$11,500,000	373	647
10	Re/Max	$10,910,330	3,725	7,841
11	Wendy's	$10,300,000	5,769	6,634
12	Taco Bell	$10,145,000	6,446	6,849
13	Hilton	$9,650,000	244	578
14	Dunkin Donuts	$9,192,000	9,141	12,538
15	Hyatt	$8,750,000	527	719

a Top 200 US Franchisors (2020). *Franchise Times*. http://www.franchisetimes.com/Top200

between 25% and 30% of revenue from international activities. Almost three-fourths of respondents said they planned to start or accelerate international ventures.[22]

Franchising Business Models

Over the years, the franchising business model has continued to develop but remains dynamic. The International Franchise Association describes two types of franchising business models that are standard within the franchise industry: Business Format franchises and Product Distribution franchises.[23] Because each type has unique characteristics, it is vital to understand the differences between them.

Business Format franchising is the most common and recognizable form of franchising. In a business format franchise, the franchisor supplies the franchisee with a trade name, products, and services. A business format franchisee can expect to receive site selection support, operating manuals, training, operating standards, marketing, and support services from the franchisor. Brands such as KFC, McDonald's, Marriott, LA Fitness, Dunkin, and Burger King are examples of such franchises.

A major strength of a business format franchise is the comparative ease in starting up a franchise brand compared to a product distribution franchise. Because of this, the business format franchise model predominates in terms of franchise brands. There are typically many different franchisors in each business category. Each of these franchisors works to distinguish itself from the others in the same business category. For example, there are over 65 home care franchise companies vying for the same candidates; one of the diligence items prospective franchisees need to investigate is how one brand differs from another.

Less common and more complex is the traditional or product distribution franchise, though it covers more total sales than business format franchising, the method and focus of doing business are primarily products manufactured or supplied by the franchisor. This business model is more complex and requires franchisees to have access to substantial capital compared to most business format franchises. The franchisee's investment in a Coca-Cola bottling plant or a Honda dealership will dwarf the amount of investment required for a typical business format franchise. In most but not all situations, the manufactured products require presale and postsale services, such as those in the automotive industry. Examples of traditional or product distribution franchising include beverage bottling, gasoline, automotive, and other manufacturing businesses.

One disadvantage of this type of franchise is the amount of investment required, a fact that limits the pool of potential franchisees. Conversely, this type of franchise attracts well-capitalized and more astute business people who have the wherewithal to operate these businesses which tend to generate a greater return.

Impact of Franchising in the United States

Franchising contributes to the economic growth of the United States by shaping its gross domestic product (GDP) and job markets. According to the International Franchise Association, 3,000 franchise brands and its 733,000 franchise establishments support nearly 7.6 million direct jobs, $674.3 billion of economic output for the U.S. economy, and 2.5% of the GDP.[24]

Franchising indirectly influences our daily activities. Each day we buy food and services from franchise businesses, stay at franchise hotels, or use a franchisor to supply senior services to our aging parents. For many people, franchising remains a reasonable business opportunity. Some have the capital to invest millions of dollars in franchise restaurants or hotels, while others buy a franchise that supplies children's or handyman services.

Advantages and Disadvantages of Franchising for Franchisors

Although franchising is a significant growth strategy for entrepreneurs, it is not free of drawbacks. Its strengths, if poorly managed, can quickly turn into disadvantages. Indeed, for many companies that decide to expand via franchising, growth comes slowly. A recent study of emerging franchisors found that a number of new brands had difficulty growing past the early stages and ceased operations altogether. It can take time for many franchisor startups to achieve even modest growth. For example, 30.6% of franchisors had only one franchise location after 4 years of operation, and after 10 years, 52.4% of that group had 50 or fewer locations.[25] These results suggest that entrepreneurs carefully consider the pros and cons of franchising before taking the plunge.

There are two primary advantages to franchising that academic scholars want to investigate.[26] Franchising allows franchisors to achieve faster growth by franchisees utilizing their capital, managerial skills, and local knowledge, allowing franchisors to build faster growth in locations, resulting in brand recognition and improving the efficiency of their business operations.

The other advantage is that franchising enables motivated and qualified entrepreneurs to administer multiple units more effectively. Franchisees are responsible for recruiting, hiring, and managing their staff. Because of the reduced cost of direct monitoring, a franchisor can maintain a more straightforward, less costly, and smaller management team.[27]

Other advantages of franchising include the following:

- Strong brand recognition: With few exceptions, a franchise network is the fastest method of building strong brand recognition. Franchisee funding enables a franchisor and its franchisees to maximize the use and effectiveness of advertising dollars. Franchisees are generally established in the community, either on a personal level or because of business activities that can provide a significant advantage in gaining local business for the franchise. Living within the franchise territory and making a permanent commitment are attributes of enormous value in helping franchisees penetrate their local markets.
- Commitment: By investing in and owning a franchise, a franchise is committed to the operation and success of its business. As franchisees invest their own capital, they do not require the supervision needed for company employees.

However, these advantages may quickly dissipate if franchisors do not carefully manage the franchising process. Franchising expertise is needed to effectively and lawfully sell franchises, train franchisees, get franchisees to ramp quickly, and focus on franchisee profitability. Without franchising guidance and qualified staff, it is easy for the franchisor to sell to the wrong franchisees, have franchisees fail, or end up with negative franchisee–franchisor relationships.

Franchising may result in a loss of control for franchisors. Despite contracts and incentive structures designed to govern the management of their units, franchisees are independent business owners who have unique local knowledge and their own views about running a business. Some franchisees may resist potential changes or oversight by franchisors, making it challenging to introduce new products, services, or marketing programs.

The state of franchise relations (which refers to the trust and mutual success between a franchisor and a franchisee) is essential for both parties. History has proven that a successful franchise program is based on enabling and supporting franchisees in realizing financial goals. If franchisees do not achieve their financial expectations, they may hold the franchisor responsible. They will look to the franchisor for answers and expect help. A poor franchisee relationship is thus one of the primary reasons for problems down the road. Unlike a corporate employee, a franchisee cannot be fired; an explicit process must be followed to terminate a franchise, one that can result in acrimony between franchisees and negative publicity for the franchisor. Other problems can include the following:

- The threat of litigation: A franchisee can threaten litigation that places a franchisor in an awkward position, making their decisions more difficult.

- Limited ability to motivate: A highly successful franchisee may become complacent and challenging to motivate, especially in mature and highly successful franchise systems. In such cases, a franchisor's options are limited but include reacquiring the franchise rights or employing various tactics to motivate the franchise.
- Limit new development: Some franchisees are concerned about threats from new franchisees within the same system. When a new franchise appears near an existing territory, a bad relationship can develop between franchises.

Advantages and Disadvantages of Franchising for Franchisees

For franchisees, there are advantages and disadvantages of owning one or multiple franchise units. One advantage lies in avoiding the risks and costs that accompany building a business from scratch. Many small startups have problems launching a brand, managing a business, creating an efficient operational structure, and finding adequate capital to fund a company. Buying franchise units is often a safer alternative.[28] Next, we have listed some advantages of buying franchise units.

- Brand recognition: In most cases, depending on the age and size of the franchise, a franchise is a recognized brand. An independent startup begins with no brand recognition.
- Marketing and sales programs: A franchise offer marketing techniques, promotional plans, and advertising materials that the franchisee does not have to create.
- Management and leadership experience: A sound franchise system will supply its franchisees with leadership and management experience, unlike an independent business where entrepreneurs must rely on their own management experience.
- Opportunity for expansion: For franchises that are successful and capable, there is the potential to expand their franchise holdings.
- Resale potential: A franchise that's part of a successful franchise system has more resale potential than many independent businesses.
- Proven operating system: A franchise does not have to set up a new operating system because the franchise will already have one. There is the added benefit of not having to invent the wheel, i.e., repeat the mistakes a franchisor has already made.
- Training and support: A franchise will supply training and, in most cases, ongoing support.
- Low overhead: Compared to an independent business, a franchise will generally have lower operating expenses.

- Cooperation from the franchise system: When franchisees create and suggest new products or services, these can benefit the entire franchise network (most new product ideas introduced by McDonald's came from its franchisees).

Still, there are potential disadvantages to buying a franchise business. An individual who invests in a franchise is putting his or her capital at risk, just like any business venture. The most significant disadvantage is the fact that a franchisee is dependent on the growth and performance of the whole network. If a franchise network does not grow, the brand may become weak. A poorly performing franchise system can have negative consequences for individual franchisees. Next, we have listed the potential disadvantages of owning a franchise.

- Buying a flawed franchise: Some franchises have flaws that can lead to failure. Like any business venture, there is a risk to franchising.
- Lack of franchisor support: As a franchise depends on support and guidance from the franchisor, a lack of these services can negatively affect the franchise.
- An unproven franchise: Investing in a startup that lacks a history of performance can be a risky proposition. A franchisor that lacks experience may have trouble deciding which way to turn.
- The franchisor focuses on selling more franchises: Some franchisors are more concerned with selling new franchises than supporting and developing existing franchisees. Whether this is driven by the need for more fees or the desire to be the most extensive system in their category, such a strategy can hurt existing franchisees.
- A franchise may be restrictive and confining. Individuals who are naturally creative and ambitious may find the requirements of a franchise stifling. Because a franchise rests upon a known operating model, such limits can frustrate independent-minded individuals.

Investing in a franchise requires thorough due diligence: Failure to carefully evaluate a franchise opportunity may place franchise investment at risk. Because some franchisors aggressively market and sell their franchises, prospective franchisees need to exercise comprehensive due diligence or suffer the consequences.

Franchise Industry Statistics

For students of franchising, it is essential to understand the types of businesses that comprise the franchise industry, system size, growth, and investment. A methodology is needed to analyze and identify the popularity and growth of franchise businesses based upon the products and services they provide. The IFA categorizes types of franchise businesses by establishing ten major franchise sectors. This classification system may be used to track business performance and growth by the type of franchise business. Currently, other entities and franchise trade publications, including *Entrepreneur* magazine and research firms Franchise Grade and Frandata, categorize franchises into sectors, with each sector covering individual franchise businesses. For example, the Quick-Serve Restaurant Sector is broken into fast food or takeout food franchises and includes such categories as Hamburger, Chicken, and Pizza. The Retail Products Sector includes retail franchises that sell products such as electronics, garden equipment, flowers, and gift stores, while franchises such as automobile dealerships, soft drink distributorships, and similar product-based formats are excluded from the franchise sectors by the IFA and the other franchise market research firms. The ten franchise sectors and the bases for including franchises categories into each sector are discussed next.

Automotive

This sector includes franchise categories that provide services pertaining to automobiles, trucks, and other motor vehicles. Notable brands include Christian Brothers Automotive, MAACO, Midas, and Jiffy Lube.

Commercial and Residential Services

This sector includes various franchise categories that include services for office buildings and homeowners. Examples include Service Master, California Closets, Mr. Rooter, Paul Davis Restoration, and Rainbow International LLC.

Quick-Service Restaurants

This is the largest franchise sector and includes locations where customers order food for takeout or sit-down dining. QSR franchises require customers to order directly without table service. Well-known franchise brands include McDonald's, Subway, Burger King, Dairy Queen, and Taco Bell.

Full-Service Restaurants

This sector includes restaurants and other establishments primarily engaged in providing food services to patrons who order and are served by waiters/waitresses. Brands include Fridays, Captain D's, Potbelly Franchising, Buffalo Wild Wings, and Hooters.

Retail Food

This sector includes retail food and beverage stores. Recognized brands include 7-Eleven, Circle-K, and AM/PM.

Lodging

This sector is sometimes referred to as the Hospitality Sector and includes hotels, motels, and other accommodations. Examples of well-known franchise brands include Marriott, Holiday Inn, Red Roof Inns, and Hilton Hotels.

Real Estate

This sector includes real estate, real estate agents, and brokers. Franchises include Century 21 Real Estate, Re/Max, and Coldwell Banker.

Retail Products and Services

This sector includes a variety of products used by customers. These products can also be found in nonfranchised businesses such as department and small retail businesses. Franchise brands include Ace Hardware, GNC, Merle Norman Cosmetics, and Hobby Town.

Business Services

This sector provides a variety of services that businesses utilize in the operation of their business. Franchise examples include FASTSIGNS, The UPS Store, Pop-A-Lock, Murphy Business, NerdsToGo, and Financial Services and Action Coach.

Personal Services

This sector has emerged as one of the fastest-growing franchise sectors and consists of services that are provided to individuals. Personal services include 24-Hour Fitness, Visiting Angels, Great Clips, Sylvan Learning Centers, and Planet Fitness.

Within these ten sectors, franchise growth and investment are dominated by different types of franchise systems.[29] An industry report analyzing FDDs of 2,154 franchise systems from 2010 to 2016 indicated that only 4% of franchise systems have 1,000 locations or more, 3% of

Table 1.3 Franchise Systems by Number of Locations[a]

Franchise Locations	Percent of Total
1,001+	4%
501–1,000	3%
101–500	21%
51–100	13%
26–50	13%
6–25	20%
0–5	25%

a Lefler, J. (2017). Diamonds in the Rough Emerging Brands
  with Potential. Franchisegrade.com

franchise systems have 501–1,000 locations, while 71% of franchise systems have 100 or fewer locations. This observation echoes the symbiosis perspective[30] we mentioned earlier, illustrating why many firms choose to stay small and grow through company-operated outlets so they can maintain ownership while deterring the free-riding of franchisees and protecting franchise reputation.

Such size disparity does not mean that only the large franchise systems receive all the attention of franchisees. Indeed, there is a significant amount of money invested in small franchise systems: over $10.7 billion was invested in franchises with 25 outlets or less, and franchises with five or fewer outlets received $3.8 billion in franchise investments. For the entrepreneur considering franchising their business, these data indicate a pool of prospective investors for smaller franchise systems (Table 1.3).

The franchise businesses that have had the most impact on franchising are seen in the following table. The rank of ten franchise sectors by the percent of franchises. The data are from 2020.

From the early stages of the modern franchise era up to the current time, Quick-Serve Restaurants, commonly referred to as fast food, has dominated the franchise industry. Over the past decade Personal Services, which include personal fitness, home care services, and children's services, has risen to the number one position in number of franchisees (Table 1.4).

Summary

We have defined franchising and delineated its history and development. We have also highlighted the economic impact of franchising and the corresponding advantages and disadvantages for both franchisors and franchisees. We presented data on the types of franchise businesses by sector and category, and the degree of franchise investment over a 6-year period.

Table 1.4 The Percent of Franchises by Franchise Sector as of 2020[a]

Personal services	27.4%
Quick-service restaurants	20.2%
Commercial and residential services	13.6%
Business services	9.0%
Retail products and services	8.3%
Full-service restaurants	7%
Automotive	4%
Retail food	4%
Lodging	3.5%
Real estate	2.9%
Total	*100%*

a Franchise Grade (2021). *The State of Emerging Franchises.* https:// assets.franchisegrade.com/files/reports/analysis-emerging-franchises_3.pdf

Franchising strategy has grown into a dynamic business model and continues to generate growth and interest for individual franchisees, private equity firms, and independent business owners who see franchising as a vehicle for propelling their small business experience into a highly successful system. Such strategy has been studied by management scholars going back to the late 1960s, when Oxenfeldt and Kelly first proposed how franchising might serve as an essential growth strategy to address resource scarcity issues for new ventures in the early stages.[31] Since then, an increasing amount of research has examined franchising strategy and its antecedents and consequences.[32] This body of research has yet to be introduced to general audiences, particularly entrepreneurs who wish to adopt a franchising strategy or purchase franchise units. To fill this gap, the following chapters delineate vital aspects of franchising that are data-driven, research-backed, and experience-tested.

Notes

1 Franchise Business Outlook (February 18, 2021).
  https://www.franchise.org/franchise-information/franchise-business-outlook/franchise-business-economic-outlook-2021
2 The Value of Franchising (2019). *Oxford Economics.*
  https://www.oxfordeconomics.com/recent-releases/The-value-of-franchising
3 Oxenfeldt, A. R., & Kelly, A. O. (1969). Will successful franchise systems ultimately become wholly owned chains? *Journal of Retailing, 44*(4), 69–83.
4 Combs, J. G., Ketchen Jr., D. J., & Short, J. C. (2011). Franchising research: Major milestones, new directions, and its future within entrepreneurship. *Entrepreneurship Theory and Practice, 35*(3), 413–425. Dant, R. P., Grünhagen, M., & Windsperger, J. (2011). Franchising research frontiers for the twenty-first century. *Journal of Retailing, 87*(3), 253–268.

5 Combs, J. G., & Ketchen Jr., D. J. (1999). Can capital scarcity help agency theory explain franchising? Revisiting the capital scarcity hypothesis. *Academy of Management Journal, 42*(2), 196–207. Falbe, C. M., & Welsh, D. H. (1998). NAFTA and franchising: A comparison of franchisor perceptions of characteristics associated with franchisee success and failure in Canada, Mexico, and the United States. *Journal of Business Venturing, 13* (2), 151–171.

6 Norton, S. W. (1988). An empirical look at franchising as an organizational form. *Journal of Business, 61*(2), 197. Shane, S. A. (1998). Making new franchise systems work. *Strategic Management Journal, 19*(7), 697–707. Combs, J. G., & Ketchen Jr., D. J. (2003). Why do firms use franchising as an entrepreneurial strategy? A meta-analysis. *Journal of Management, 29*(3), 443–465.

7 Shane, S. A. (1996). Why franchise companies expand overseas. *Journal of Business Venturing, 11*(2), 73–88. Lafontaine, F. (1992). Agency theory and franchising: Some empirical results. *RAND Journal of Economics, 23*(2), 263–283.

8 Bradach, J. L., & Eccles, R. G. (1989). Price, authority, and trust: From ideal types to plural forms. *Annual Review of Sociology,* 97–118. Perryman, A. A., & Combs, J. G. (2012). Who should own it? An agency-based explanation for multi-outlet ownership and co-location in plural form franchising. *Strategic Management Journal, 33*(4), 368–386.

9 Hendrikse, G., Hippmann, P., & Windsperger, J. (2015). Trust, transaction costs and contractual incompleteness in franchising. *Small Business Economics, 44*(4), 867–888. Kosová, R., & Sertsios, G. (2016). An empirical analysis of self-enforcement mechanisms: Evidence from hotel franchising. *Management Science, 64*(1), 43–63.

10 Levenson, S., & Joseph, F. (1969). *China – An Interpretive History: From the Beginnings to the Fall of Han.* Regents of the University of California, London, England.

11 Hisrich, R., Peters, M., & Shepherd, D. (2016). *Entrepreneurship.* McGraw-Hill Education.

12 Seid, M.H. *Where It All Began. The Evolution of Franchising.* http://www.franchise-chat.com/resources/where_it_all_began_the_evolution_of_franchising.htm

13 Love, J. F., & Miller, A. W. (1986). *McDonald's: Behind the Arches.* Bantam Books, New York.

14 Feloni, R. (2015). KFC founder Colonel Sanders didn't achieve his remarkable rise to success until his 60s. *Business Insider.* https://amp.businessinsider.com/how-kfc-founder-colonel-sanders-achieved-success-in-his-60s-2015-6

15 Teixeira, E. (2018). The enigma of the emerging franchise. *Forbes.* https://www.forbes.com/sites/edteixeira/2018/04/11/the-enigma-of-the-emerging-franchise/#171c04d61268

16 7-Year Longitudinal Study of Franchise Industry (2017). *FranchiseGrade.* https://www.franchisegrade.com/reports/article/7-year-longitudinal-study

17 Pitegoff, T. (2015). Some multi-unit franchisees are public companies. *Franchise Alchemy.* https://franchisealchemy.com/some-multi-unit-franchisees-are-public-companies/

18 Franchise Rule (1978). *Federal Trade Commission.* https://www.ftc.gov/enforcement/rules/rulemaking-regulatory-reform-proceedings/franchise-rule

19 The international franchise association – Celebrating 50 years of dedicated service to franchising (2010). *International Franchise Association*. https://www.franchise.org/the-international-franchise-association%E2%80%94-celebrating-50-years-of-dedicated-service-to-franchising

20 The Coalition of Franchisee Associations (2016). https://thecfainc.com/about-us/cfa-history/

21 Boll, R. (2016). Top markets report franchising a market assessment tool for U.S. exporters. *U.S. Department of Commerce – International Trade Administration*. https://www.trade.gov/topmarkets/pdf/Franchising_Top_Markets_Report.pdf

22 U.S. Commercial Service Franchising. https://2016.export.gov/industry/franchising/index.asp

23 International Franchise Association (2016). https://www.franchise.org/what-is-a-franchise

24 International Franchise Association (2020). https://franchiseeconomy.com/about/

25 Teixeira, E., & Olson, S. (2017). *The State of Emerging Franchise Systems Part 1*. https://assets.franchisegrade.com/files/reports/analysis_of_emerging_franchises.pdf

26 Combs, J. G., Ketchen Jr., D. J., & Short, J. C. (2011). Franchising research: Major milestones, new directions, and its future within entrepreneurship. *Entrepreneurship Theory and Practice, 35*(3), 413–425.

27 Combs, J. G., & Ketchen Jr., D. J. (2003). Why do firms use franchising as an entrepreneurial strategy? A meta-analysis. *Journal of Management, 29*(3), 443–465.

28 Hisrich, R., Peters, M., & Shepherd, D. (2016). *Entrepreneurship*. McGraw-Hill Education.

29 Lefler, J. (2017). *Diamonds in the Rough Emerging Brands with Potential*. Franchisegrade.com

30 Bradach, J. L., & Eccles, R. G. (1989). Price, authority, and trust: From ideal types to plural forms. *Annual Review of Sociology*, 97–118. Perryman, A. A., & Combs, J. G. (2012). Who should own it? An agency-based explanation for multi-outlet ownership and co-location in plural form franchising. *Strategic Management Journal, 33*(4), 368–386.

31 Oxenfeldt, A. R., & Kelly, A. O. (1968). Will successful franchise systems ultimately become wholly owned chains? *Journal of Retailing, 44*, 69–83.

32 Rosado-Serrano, A., Paul, J., & Dikova, D. (2018). International franchising: A literature review and research agenda. *Journal of Business Research, 85*, 238–257.

Chapter 2

Fundamentals of Franchising

In the previous chapter, we introduced the concept of franchising strategy, delineated its key rhetorical framework and history, and presented economic impacts and relevant data. In this chapter, we delve deeper into the fundamentals of franchising, focusing on essential components of the franchise model.

The Components of the Franchise Business Model

In its purest form, the franchise business model consists of a franchisee acquiring the rights to use the trademarks and operating system of the franchiser by paying an initial franchise fee and remitting a continuous fee or royalty based on a percentage of the operating revenue or profit. A franchise consists of specific components that make the franchise business model unique. Many of these components are critical for all franchise systems and may significantly determine the performance of franchise systems spanning several market spaces. While all of these aspects are valuable, we will discuss the most critical next.

Franchise Intellectual Property

Franchise Intellectual Property (IP) refers to the property category of creations by humans that underlie the operation of a franchise business.[1] IP may be separated from individual entrepreneurs and traded in the open market,[2] making it an effective tool to protect and transfer the value of a franchiser's intangible assets, which represent the investment that franchisers make in designing and building a franchise and its operating system. The primary forms of IP are copyright, trademark, patents, and trade secrets. Franchisers have IP rights in the areas of brands, copyrights for training and promotional materials, and patents for proprietary inventions. The protection of IP rights is essential to all franchise businesses. Franchisers use tools such as nondisclosure and noncompete agreements, and when necessary, litigation to protect their IP.

DOI: 10.4324/9781003034285-2

IP is an important component of the franchise business model because it contributes to the success of the franchise system by defining the brands, logos, and other aspects that customers associate with that franchise.[3] It also delineates a franchise system'system to determine if the operating system is properly integrated and to make necessary adjustment key strategic assets, particularly those related to its business operation and technology capability. It may be used to connect the franchise brand to the customer (i.e., McDonald's Golden Arches). The franchise operations manual is an important example of IP as it describes and contains key information pertaining to the operation of that franchise. For these reasons, it's important for a franchise system to maintain a competitive advantage by protecting its IP from other companies, franchisers, and franchisees.

Franchisers need to ensure that key operating ingredients and proprietary knowledge remain confidential in order to prevent others from utilizing it, as well as avoid confusion on the part of customers. Examples of IP protections include the secret Coca-Cola formula and KFC's recipe for fried chicken. Franchisers protect their IP by relying on nondisclosure, confidentiality, and noncompete agreements.

Other IP protection steps include using a watch service, companies that notify a client if it receives trademark information from the government, misuse on the internet that match or could infringe on the trademark, and the use of IP by another company. However, dispersion of a franchiser's IP in manuals, online and in other locations, may leave it vulnerable to misuse or theft by unscrupulous individuals or disgruntled franchisees. Protecting IP requires constant policing by the franchiser, which includes having their legal counsel continually take steps to strengthen a franchiser's rights to IP, as contained in their franchise agreements and ancillary documents.

The Franchise Trade/Service

The Franchise Trade/Service represents a major part of a franchiser's IP. These consist of recognizable words, phrases, names, slogans, or logos that distinguish products or services of a franchise from its competitors.[4] Trademarks represent the foundation of a franchise system since they identify and differentiate the brand, its products, and services from other franchises and independent businesses. A franchise trademark is so important that it is considered its most asset; because of the importance of trademarks to businesses, federal and state governments have procedures and regulations for registering and protecting trademark rights.

The value and use of a franchise trademark may be enhanced by effective marketing strategies, including the use of a catchy or attractive slogan and price promotions. Some of the most memorable franchise slogans include KFC (It's finger lickin' good), Coca-Cola (Open Happiness), Dunkin' Donuts (America runs on Dunkin'), and McDonald's (I'm lovin' it).

Another strategy is to tie a trademark to the decor and design of a franchise location. The colors and design of a franchise trademark and logo should relate to the components of a franchise's products or services. Businesses invest considerable resources in developing their brands so that consumers recognize and distinguish their products and services from others. Federal and state trademark protections are intended to stop infringement of the rights of trademark owners and their authorized users (such as franchisees) and to serve the public interest by preventing consumer confusion.[5]

All trademarks are brands but not all brands are trademarks. The franchise brand is what the public sees, while a trademark is a distinct aspect of the brand that signals not only a particular standardization of the franchise system but carries legal protection because it is a unique identifier for the franchise.[6] A franchise trademark is a valuable tool to promote and advertise a franchise system. These identifiers should result in customer expectations of product/service quality with their use in marketing, advertising, and promotional programs. If customers receive quality products and services, they will relate that positive experience to franchise trade and service marks. Conversely, a negative customer experience will result in a poor association with trade and service marks.

The impact of a franchise trademark is maximized when it is associated with a quality franchise system. A strong franchise trademark can deliver loyalty, stability, and recurring revenue for the franchiser and franchisees. A study using data from the restaurant and motel industries found empirical evidence showing that franchising offsets the problems that nonfranchise companies face when their outlets are widely dispersed among markets with brand name capital.[7] Franchising can increase brand name capital and the development of larger local outlets compared to nonfranchised operations.

Registration of the franchise trademark is an important process that should be done by a qualified trademark attorney who can do a trademark search and properly register the trademark, slogans, and logos. When registering a trademark, it's important to consider future products and services that might be offered under the trademark. Avoid cost-cutting by using so-called inexpensive online legal services.

It is essential that franchisers protect their brand and trademark by constantly enforcing franchise standards among their franchisees.[8] When franchisers fail to uphold system standards, the result can be irreparable harm to the brand and the franchisees. If a franchiser fails to take appropriate steps to protect its brand, lax enforcement of franchise standards may lead to damaging outcomes for the franchiser, franchises and, most importantly, the value of the franchise brand. The brand is so crucial to the operation of a franchise system that most franchisers do not hesitate to take legal action in order to protect it.

The Franchise Operating System

The Franchise Operating System refers to standardized processes and policies which the franchisee must follow in order to manage, market, and operate a franchise. The franchise operating system is another part of franchise IP and is what sets the franchising business model apart from other businesses.[9] It prescribes the formula for how a franchisee should operate their franchise units in a consistent manner, and represents a compilation of processes which, in combination, can result in a successful franchise operation. The operating system includes such details as opening hours, store appearance, sanitation requirements, suggested retail pricing, authorized products and services, employee job descriptions, financial obligations, compliance with regulatory authorities, food menus, recipes and ingredients, and other activities that are integral to the daily operation of a franchise. When properly designed and successfully executed, the operating system provides a franchise with the ingredients to achieve franchise profitability. Startup and emerging franchisers should measure performance in order to identify the effectiveness of their operating system to determine if the operating system is properly integrated and to make necessary adjustments.

The elements of a franchise operating system are essential to the success of a franchise because when properly followed, franchisees can deliver the franchise products/services with consistent quality that meet consumer expectations regardless of the franchise location.[10] Chick-Fil-a, McDonald's, Burger King, and Marriott Hotels are notable franchises with operating systems that result in a consistent consumer experience across various locations.

By being documented in training manuals, written procedures, and franchiser bulletins, the operating system can be used to enforce franchise system compliance. Without an operating system, the essence of a franchise system is diminished since it will fail to prescribe the guidelines for operating the business.

If franchisees believe that the franchise operating system is flawed, this may negatively affect feedback that existing franchisees provide to candidates and slow system growth. Examples of a flawed franchise operating system can include the types of products or services that franchises must offer, unnecessary staffing requirements that increase operating expenses, and lengthy hours of operation.

Adherence to the operating system is essential in order to protect the franchise brand. When the operating system is not followed, it may damage the reputation of the franchise brand. Franchisers try to effect compliance by auditing locations, using mystery shoppers who visit as customers, and requiring franchisees to follow all franchise systems and procedures. Another way to achieve compliance is to use legal safeguards for franchise operating standards as cited in the franchise agreement. Litigation can be an effective way to make franchisees aware of why it is vital that all franchisees follow the operating system, and encourage franchisees to police franchise compliance whenever possible.

Franchisers can improve and enhance the quality and effectiveness of their operating systems through feedback obtained from franchisees on a regular basis. The use of franchise advisory committees is another method to gain input from franchisees on how to improve a franchise operating system.

Franchise Training

Franchise Training refers to educational and instructive programs designed to teach and improve the efficiency and effectiveness of franchisees and their employees in operating a franchise system.[11] Franchisee training may consist of a franchisee classroom and onsite training, franchiser bulletins, newsletters, webinars, conferences, and annual conventions. The initial training that a new franchisee receives is critical to prepare them to set up and operate a franchise for the first time. This means it's essential that new franchisees receive quality training before they open their franchise. Without quality training, it can be costly and time-consuming for a franchisee to be retrained and may require the franchiser to frequently respond to questions and requests for assistance. A franchise training program reflects the commitment of a franchiser to build a successful operation of its franchise and signals the quality of knowledge transfer between franchiser and its franchisees.

Given its vital role in transferring operating knowledge to franchisees, the Federal Trade Commission requires that a detailed description of the initial franchisee training program is included in the Franchise Disclosure Document. This description must include what the training represents in terms of topics, number of training hours, manuals, and the title of the person teaching each subject.

Franchisee training curriculums may vary, depending upon the age and size of the franchise system and its location.[12] Some startup franchises begin with a modest training staff that includes the franchise founder as a key presenter. More mature franchisers will provide a more comprehensive training presentation that can include more specialized franchise staff. The quality of an initial franchisee training program will depend upon what franchiser resources are applied to the training. Franchise training is an iterative process, and franchisers should be willing to commit sufficient resources based on feedback from new and existing franchisees regarding the quality and effectiveness of training. The more franchisee training programs, the greater will be the opportunity to gain feedback on the effectiveness of the training. Post franchisee interviews, training evaluations completed at the end of each day, and a Q&A from the presenter regarding training sessions are ways to help provide timely and quality feedback on training subjects and presentations. An example of a comprehensive franchisee training is that provided by Paul Pickett, Chief Development Officer for Wild Birds Unlimited, a franchise brand recognized for its successful program, who says, "At Wild Birds Unlimited, we provide 18 hours of online training focusing on financial management, customer service and product knowledge prior to the full week of classroom training at our Franchise Support Center. Franchisees then spend a week of in-store training at a Certified Training Store to learn how to implement those operational best practices."

One of the most important requirements of an initial franchisee training program is scheduled training. If training is done too early, a new franchisee may not retain much of what they learned. Conversely, if the training is too late, a franchisee may make important decisions regarding staffing, equipment, vendor relationships, and marketing programs before they are fully trained.

Home-based franchises require no site location process or major equipment, so the franchise launch can be done quickly. Training should be done first and the franchisee should be ready to launch.

A franchise that is not complex may still require a separate site location. Training should be scheduled right before the franchisee has signed for the location lease. Franchise agreements usually include a rarely invoked clause, where a franchiser may fail a franchisee for not successfully completing training; thus, a franchisee who is obligated to lease before training may create a difficult situation for both parties.

Complex franchise concepts such as food, retail or lodging franchises should schedule training in stages. The first stage should include the basics of the franchise operation such as staffing, site location requirements, and vendor arrangements. After completion, the franchisee may find an acceptable site and recruit staff and vendors. Once the site is accepted by the franchiser, the next stage of training is a combination of classroom and onsite at a franchise or company location.

Franchise training is an important tool for teaching and reinforcing franchise policies, products, services, and operating procedures, and preparing franchises to implement the franchise operating system. Changes in the operating system should be preceded by proper training; otherwise, it can lead to problems in execution. When a new product or important operating policy is introduced with proper training, this will result in effective franchisee implementation. Training should include the reason for introduction of a change, the new procedure or marketing information, and a list of FAQs regarding the specific training subject.

The role of quality franchisee training in the success of franchise operations is exemplified by top-performing franchise systems. Franchise performance and franchisee satisfaction levels are directly influenced by the overall quality of franchiser training.

The Franchise Operations Manual

The Franchise Operations Manual is a critical depositary of training and franchise operating information that includes how to start and prepare a franchise to open for business. It sets forth essential components of the operating system, key franchisee obligations, and serves as a policy and training guide for franchisees. While it may not effectively prevent the disruption of a franchise system, the Manual is a pivotal component of the franchise operating system since it fulfills several essential functions, from serving as a training guide to how to recruit and hire the most qualified franchise staff.[13]

The entire Franchise Operations Manual can consist of several separate manuals including a Franchise Startup Manual, Franchise Operations Manual, and Franchise Marketing Manual. In most cases, the term Manual is used in the singular form in franchise FDDs but still refers collectively to more than one Manual. Mary Ann McConnell, President of Franwise a franchise consulting firm states that the Manuals serve four main purposes: 1. Faster and better franchise development and performance, 2. Definition and detailed compliance processes for all brand standards and contractual obligations, so franchisees know what is expected, what resources are available and how they can measure their progress, 3 Reduced strain and need for franchisor staff and 4. Franchisors can rely on the manual for legal compliance and defense.

While no Manual can save a bad franchise system, one that is well documented should be able to use its Manuals as one of the tools to stave off unfavorable rulings. A detailed Manual will also help ensure that you and your franchisees comply with all the promises and obligations of the Franchise Disclosure Document (FDD) and Franchise Agreement (FA). Marketing the detail and depth of information shown in the Table of Contents of your Operations Manual (as provided in the Franchise Disclosure Document) is a valuable marketing tool for the Franchise Development Department.

The Manual should be available in digital format for ease of delivery and to facilitate updates and important changes.

The Manual includes the standards and procedures that franchisees follow to operate their franchise and meet the expectations of the franchise brand. The Manual can include such individual manuals as

Preopening, Startup, and marketing. It provides guidance by documenting franchise policy on human resources, financial reporting, marketing, and accounting policies. It serves as a training guide, reference, and resource for franchisees. Due to its importance, the FTC requires that the table of contents from the Manual be included as an exhibit to a Franchise Disclosure Document.

Manuals may be intricate in the case of fast food and restaurant franchises, which involve unique décor and equipment standards, product ingredients, and recipes. Operations manuals can be more straightforward as in the case of personal service franchises. The less complicated a franchise operating system is, the less complex the manual will be. A Manual is an important component in franchise system compliance. If a dispute or issue arises between a franchiser and franchisee, the Manual is an important tool to settle it, since the franchiser's copy is defined as the controlling document.

Franchisers may allow prospective franchisees to view the Operations Manual before purchasing a franchise. However, since the information in an Operations Manual is deemed confidential by the franchiser, it will require that the prospect sign confidentiality and nondisclosure agreements before viewing the Manual.[14]

The contents of an Operations Manual will vary depending on the type of business, but typical issues addressed include the following:

1 The history, goal, or vision of the franchisor
2 Procedures for finding and developing a franchise location
3 Preopening procedures
4 Equipment and inventory requirements
5 Daily operating procedures
6 Administrative and reporting obligations
7 Payroll, accounting, and computer systems
8 Marketing and advertising guidelines
9 Customer service
10 Management procedures

Franchise Marketing

Franchise Marketing refers to activities and resources devoted to communicating, delivering, and exchanging goods or services with potential customers. Given that one of the most important factors in shaping the financial performance of franchise units is brand reputation, it is not surprising that marketing is a critical part of the strategy for a successful franchise. Marketing activities enable franchisees to promote and publicize a franchise brand in a consistent manner to existing and potential customers.[15] When designed and executed correctly, marketing activities can maximize franchiser productivity and franchisee advertising dollars. One of the most important objectives of franchise marketing is to build and enhance franchise brand recognition. This objective is so critical to building a successful franchise system, it can impact the development of new franchise locations, so that closely situated franchises will maximize brand recognition.

Franchise marketing includes promotional advertising, grand opening programs, creation, and production of marketing materials, public relations campaigns, and customer research. Startups and emerging franchisers should monitor the performance of a franchisee to determine whether their marketing system is coordinated. Franchise revenues can depend on the right mix of products or services, effective marketing programs, and favorable vendor arrangements. In combination, these components can deliver positive results. However, when out of sync, results can fall short of expectations.

Most franchisers require that franchisees contribute to an advertising or marketing fund in addition to franchise royalty payments. Such contributions can be fixed dollar amounts or, more commonly, a fixed percentage of franchise revenues. Some franchise agreements require the franchisee to contribute to both local and national advertising or marketing funds. Accumulated funds can be administered by the franchiser, or in the case of larger and mature franchise systems, an advertising committee. Franchise advertising committees are normally governed by franchise representatives who collectively determine and structure marketing strategies and the funds allotted. The amount of money in funds and decisions for dispensing them can become so adversarial that some large franchise systems such as Burger King and KFC have waged major litigation with franchisees. When franchisers include franchisee representatives in the marketing process, it's important that a franchiser establishes a consensus among members rather than make a unilateral major marketing decision. It's quite common for startup franchisers to forego advertising fund contributions by franchisees until they have reached a minimum number of franchisees, for example, five or ten.

A popular strategy that some franchisers employ is complementary branding, which is when an established franchise brand offers a high-quality product in order to attract customers. An established brand can capitalize on brand recognition and quality.[16] An example of complementary branding is when McDonald's added soft-serve ice cream to its menu in 1995. Soon after, quick-service restaurants such as Wendy's, Chick-fil-A and Burger King put soft-serve on their own menus. Dairy Queen used a similar strategy when it added the Brazier concept featuring hamburgers in addition to a soft-serve menu.

Despite its significant impact on the financial performance of franchise units, marketing activities can be difficult for a franchise chain to coordinate.[17] While franchisers try to gain the full participation of franchisees in an advertising program, federal antitrust statutes prevent them from mandating franchise pricing. Thus, promotional advertisements often include the disclaimer "available at participating locations only."

Franchisers strive to achieve full participation in several ways. They can educate franchisees about the need to participate in price promotions by stressing the importance of presenting a consistent experience to customers, regardless of location. Alternatively, they may engage franchisee participation via marketing committees or other means. Some franchisers use advertising to obtain pricing compliance by making customers aware of advertised prices, which can cause a franchise to follow them. As an example, national advertising programs have been shown to significantly improve the performance of franchisee units.[18]

Marketing strategies are often based on the creative contributions of an advertising or public relations firm. Because of the creative nature of certain marketing tactics, it is not unusual for those involved in the process to have an opinion. To avoid confrontation and gain support for certain marketing and price promotion programs, franchisers should first test the strategy in several franchise locations. This process serves two functions: to test the efficacy of the marketing program; and if successful, gain the advocacy of the franchisees who participated in the test or pilot program.

Franchise Development

Franchise Development refers to the recruitment of qualified franchisee candidates and the sale of new franchises. It includes activities required to build and grow the franchise system. The development of new franchise units is the engine that powers a franchise system to achieve rapid revenue growth, brand recognition, and market acquisition. For a franchise startup, it's important that development activities commence as quickly as possible. Selling a first franchise can be a challenge for some startups, requiring that franchise development be properly organized and staffed. Franchise development provides the assets necessary to support the business model, research and develop new products and services, and strengthen the foundation of the franchise system. Failure to develop a franchise system may impair the financial health of the franchiser and prevent the support and assistance that franchisees require.

To achieve franchise system growth requires the execution of certain activities including advertising to prospective franchisees, processing franchise inquiries, qualifying franchise candidates, and completing a franchise transaction.[19]

Successful franchise development requires the formation of a Franchise Disclosure Model appropriate for the franchise business model. In most cases, the single or unit franchise model is most appropriate for emerging franchises; in other cases, the multi-unit franchise may be a more effective option. This issue will be explored in subsequent chapters.

The franchise development process begins with an initial contact between the candidate and the franchise representative. Franchise candidates should be profiled, recruited, qualified, and guided through the franchising process. Whether the initial contact is by email, social media, or telephone, it's important that the representative respond as quickly as possible. The person communicating with the franchisee should have a sales personality, be familiar with the basics of the franchise program, and careful to gather key information from prospective franchisees. Since many franchisers utilize an automated telephone response and directory system, it is critical that prospective franchisees speak directly to a representative, or receive a return call as soon as possible. Franchise staff should present the advantages of a franchise program and respond to any concerns and questions from prospective franchisees.

In addition to recruitment, in order to properly develop a successful franchise network, the franchise must have a competent staff that can effectively screen and pre-qualify candidates. The selection process is vital to the success of a franchise system[20] and should start with a careful understanding of the knowledge, skills, and abilities that enable franchisees to successfully duplicate a business model. Further, the selection process should ensure a value alignment between potential franchisees and franchisers, which can not only reduce relationship conflicts but also boost the performance of the franchise system.[21]

Franchise staff should present the advantages of the program and respond to the concerns and questions of prospective franchisees. A successful franchise development program depends on franchisees giving it a positive evaluation so it is important to maintain a satisfying and mutually beneficial relationship with existing franchisees since a dissatisfied franchisee can spread negative feedback among prospective franchisees. When obtaining the feedback of existing franchisees, a franchisee training program is a significant part of the evaluation process. If franchise training is evaluated poorly by existing franchisees, a prospective franchisee may decide not to invest in that franchise.

Franchiser Support

Franchiser Support is defined as the collective help, resources, advice, leadership, and operational support that a franchiser supplies to franchisees. Franchise support is vital because it enables a franchisee to improve its operation. A lack of franchiser support is one of the major issues that hinder a franchisee's chance of success.[22] Franchise support is critical, especially when franchisees encounter operating problems or experience a shortfall in revenue. It is important that franchisers respond to a franchisee's earnest request for help, regardless of how much help a franchiser is contractually bound to provide. When a franchiser does not respond to a legitimate request for help or support, this may lead to franchisee dissatisfaction, disputes, and possibly litigation. Franchise support is especially important for franchisees who have less experience as looking for resources to help them navigate unfamiliar business environments.[23] Franchise field consultants are the most common source of support. They often make site visits to assigned locations, audit the performance of franchisees, and recommend approaches to improve a franchise's success. The amount of franchiser support, including number and frequency of visits, is defined in the franchise agreement so that obligations of the franchiser and expectations of franchisees are clearly understood.

Franchiser support will vary, depending upon the type of franchise system, something that is often industry specific. Hotel, motel, and food franchises are often complex by virtue of the number and type of services they provide. They are among the most needy franchise systems in terms of franchiser support. Medical staffing franchises, children's educational services, and residential services require less oversight because their business models are less complex.[24]

Because a significant benefit of the franchise model is providing franchisees an established and proven operating system, it is incumbent upon franchisers to diagnose the causes of poor performance, in order to identify those franchisees in need of support and assistance to correct their problems. A franchiser should survey franchisees on a regular basis to determine if they are satisfied with the level of franchiser support and services they are receiving. A franchiser should carefully manage the relationship with current franchisees, as active communication between franchisor and franchisee will help strengthen trust and satisfaction with the franchise system.[25] Some franchisers provide franchisees with a troubleshooting guide or list of FAQs to assist them when they encounter a problem that requires franchiser assistance. FAQs should include a list of franchiser staff to contact for reporting specific problems and issues.

Mitch Cohen, a principal in Perfomax Franchise Advisors and a multi-unit franchisee, states that proper franchiser assistance is determined by franchiser leadership, a trait common to great franchise brands. Franchisees expect a franchiser to exercise leadership, have a vision for the future, and share their brand strategy with franchisees. These attributes are ingredients of effective franchiser support.

Vendor Purchasing Programs

Vendor Purchasing Programs refer to arrangements made by franchisers with vendors for the procurement of marketing materials, menu ingredients, products for resale, equipment, fixtures, point of sale equipment, and certain services used by a franchisee in the operation of their business. An effective vendor purchasing program enables franchisees to purchase equipment, products, services, and supplies at discounted prices. Franchisers use vendor purchasing programs to control and enforce the standards that franchisees must follow, which is particularly relevant to concepts such as fast food, restaurant, and lodging franchises.

Some vendor purchase programs include services such as insurance brokers, advertising firms, printing services, and real estate brokers used by children's tutoring services, real estate, homecare franchises, and other nonproduct franchises. Favorable franchiser vendor purchasing programs are an asset that can attract and sell new franchises when viewed as another advantage that franchise ownership provides. The financial benefits franchisees receive from vendor purchasing programs contribute to the ability of a franchise to generate profits and aggressively market and promote products and services. Franchisees may expect that one benefit of a franchise system is collective buying power on behalf of franchises. If a franchiser fails to deliver it can lead to dissatisfaction. As a franchise system grows, it's not unusual for a vendor to offer the franchiser rebates based on franchisee purchases. The dollar amount of rebates received by a franchiser must be disclosed in the FDD. Some franchisers share a portion of the rebates with their franchisees by placing the funds in an advertising or marketing fund.

The relationship between franchiser and vendor may be contractual in nature, or a vendor recommendation may be provided to franchisees. These are a significant part and benefit of the franchise model which enables the franchiser to carefully select vendors and boost its bargaining power.[26] A startup franchise with few locations will not generally attract vendors. The larger a franchise system grows, the more attractive it will be to vendors.

Vendors can be classified into two groups. The first group, Required Vendors, includes vendors a franchisee must buy from under the terms of the franchise agreement. By using Required Vendors, the franchiser can set up a reputable franchise model that supplies franchise customers with a consistent experience, regardless of which franchise they visit. Required vendor programs help both parties because franchisees can buy at lower prices and the franchiser can uphold franchise standards and more easily control the production and sale of franchise products and services. Before naming a Required Vendor, franchisers should make sure that their products meet quality standards, best pricing is available, and the vendor has a warranty or return policy.

The other group of vendors is the Recommended or Approved Vendor. These are vendors that a franchisee doesn't have to use, but if franchises do use them, they can take advantage of favorable pricing and the vendor's familiarity with the franchise program. It's rare for a franchiser in the food franchise sector, for example, to allow franchisees to purchase menu ingredients from just any vendor.

Purchasing cooperatives are one method that franchisers use to maximize the power of the franchise supply chain. Purchasing supply analysts found that a buying system can save 2%–5% in purchase savings. Franchisers and franchisees may realize a cost savings of up to 8% through a purchasing cooperative.[27] A franchiser and franchisees from the same franchise system own the purchasing cooperative which is run by a board of directors. Each member is entitled to one share ownership and any rebates or monies earned by the cooperative must be distributed to the shareholders. The franchiser keeps the right to approve or disapprove vendors and require that franchisees buy specific and proprietary products.[28]

Effective and productive franchiser supplier purchasing programs can be an asset to attract and sell new franchise locations; this is seen as another advantage that franchise ownership provides. In addition, the financial benefits that franchisees receive from supplier purchasing programs contribute to their ability to aggressively market and promote products and services.

A franchiser that has launched a new franchise should solicit input from potential vendors at the outset so that the franchiser can identify which vendors provide the best purchasing opportunities for new franchisees. This is critical for a franchise startup as new franchisees will rely on the franchiser to provide them with a list of vendors. Eventually, franchisees may utilize a vendor seeking to supply products or services to the entire franchise network, in which case the vendor's familiarity with the franchise program can be an advantage.

Competitive Intelligence

Competitive Intelligence (CI) refers to the collection, analysis, and distribution of information related to the products, customers, competitors, and environmental factors that enable franchisees to make strategic decisions. It includes competitive product and pricing knowledge, site location expertise, new product introduction, and competitive marketing practices. This is a valuable part of the franchise model that a franchiser can gather from its franchise network CI since it supplies useful information in the design and construction of the new franchise. Important components include the territory, initial franchise fee, continuing franchise fees, and initial and renewal terms to be considered when designing and constructing a new franchise program. Franchise marketing and promotional programs are enhanced and more effective when CI is available to complement the creation and execution of these programs. However, it is more difficult for franchise systems with a large number of franchised outlets to enjoy the benefits of competitive knowledge because it is costly to convince franchisees to attend to and utilize such knowledge. Systems can resolve these obstacles by promoting franchisee motivation and their ability to share, absorb, and utilize such knowledge.[29]

Since franchise system marketing can be readily accessed by competitors, lack of ongoing CI may expose a franchise system to unanticipated interruptions in revenue flows. Because franchises under the same brand can exist in multiple markets, ongoing CI can be gathered more often rather than limiting CI research to once a year. Franchisers and their franchises can capitalize on data gathering by casting a wider net that includes competitive job postings, local and regional press releases, and regional and local product promotions. By sharing among its franchise network and limiting gathering CI to a few people and departments, franchisers and franchisees can include CI as part of the agenda for marketing committees and franchise advisory councils.[30]

The collective creativity and knowledge available from a franchisee should be used to enable the gathering and flow of information between franchiser and franchisees by sharing feedback, suggestions, and ideas through webinars, conferences, and meetings where both groups can contribute. Mitch Pinckney, an accomplished franchise executive who has built a highly successful multi-unit B2B personnel/staffing company as a franchisee, spent the past 15 years as a franchise development coach and consultant. In his appraisal of CI, quality franchise companies should offer tools for marketing or run national marketing campaigns themselves. Gaining national attention is easier when a central entity (the franchiser) handles most of the promotions. It keeps the message consistent and allows brand building and integrity. Even franchises that have neither the size nor the capital to run a national marketing campaign can usually provide local franchise owners with the tools and marketing guidelines to promote their business. Together, CI and marketing research provide the necessary framework to efficiently position a franchise's products/services and establish pricing strategies based on current and projected market realities.

CI can also be a source of information regarding franchise vendors. If another franchiser utilizes certain vendors, they may meet franchise vendor specifications and as a result enhance the vendor evaluation process.

The Franchise Territory

When a franchisee signs the franchise agreement, they are granted a designated territory for the term of the franchise. Franchisers can define a franchise territory by boundaries using geographical terms such as zip code, street, city, county, or geographical features such as a highway or river, while others might use demographic data such as people over the age of 65 for a homecare franchise territory. A franchise agreement can include a sales quota or similar performance clause to protect the franchiser from a franchise not fully developing its territory.

A franchise territory may be Exclusive, Protected, or Open. Sometimes used interchangeably, such terms have different meanings in franchising.[31] When a franchise territory is Exclusive, the franchise should be the only source of products or services in the territory, but if the territory is Protected, the franchiser may be allowed to sell through channels of distribution such as the internet and certain retail outlets. In both cases, the franchiser is not allowed to franchise or open a company-run location within the designated territory.

Some franchise systems do not supply territorial protection. Under an Open Territory, the franchiser is free to open both franchise and company-owned outlets near an existing franchise location. The franchiser can use alternative channels of distribution whenever it wants. Studies have shown that Open Territory models may not always lead to poor performance of franchised units. When franchisers approve new units in the vicinity of existing units, this may reduce the incumbent's profits; however, when company-owned units open nearby, incumbents may experience an increase in their revenue,[32] perhaps because company-owned units must adhere to franchise rules and regulations and are thus less likely to cannibalize incumbents' revenue, while franchised units are more flexible, and willing to pursue strategies for local adaptation and value maximization.[33]

Richard Rosen, a prominent franchise attorney, believes that franchise companies should disclose whether there is a protected territory, but that's not the only territorial issue that a prospective franchisee may challenge. Rosen considers the territory one of the most important agreement terms to negotiate, a provision that many franchisers are willing to adjust.

Franchisers need to be cautious concerning the size of the territory they grant to a franchise. A territory that is too small can limit the efforts of an aggressive franchisee, while a territory that is too big may become underdeveloped. It is easier to add territory to a franchise than to reduce it.

The importance of franchise territory and its quality and size is one of the determining factors when a prospective franchise compares one franchise opportunity to another. The design and granting of a franchise territory are key parts of a franchise strategy to promote and maximize the brand. When a franchiser grants disjointed franchise territories in regions or markets, it may stifle brand awareness, increase costs to service and support franchisees, and diminish the productivity of marketing and advertising expenditures.

Franchise Site Selection

For franchises in the retail, restaurant, personal services, and hospitality franchise sectors, the selection and terms of a franchise location are one of the most critical components of the business model. Site selection should carefully include a number of factors, such as general location, demographics, traffic information, competition, and cost considera-tion.[34] The usage of CI, demographic data, and franchisee research can help franchisees to identify the most desirable franchise location for targeting potential customers. Franchise site location is a significant as-pect of retail and food franchise concepts, as both parties have a vested interest in identifying the best possible franchise location.[35] Because of its importance, franchisers often outsource site location services to firms specializing in that business. A potentially lucrative franchise territory may be severely diminished by the wrong location.

In some service and business-to-business franchises, site location may not be as critical because customers do not go to the location to obtain products or services. However, some franchises that are non-retail or food brands are located in light industrial areas. For example, children's recreational franchises that require large facilities such as indoor play-grounds and swimming franchises.

The importance of site selection is a high priority because it will have a direct impact on the performance of a franchisee who invests in a rental lease or building purchase, along with remodeling, fixtures, and equipment. The wrong site can be costly to correct since franchisees usually execute leases that run several years or longer. Good site location is essential to customer accessibility, convenience, and the ability of the franchisee to effectively compete against both franchised and nonfranchised businesses. Exposure to main roads is an important consideration for site location. Other businesses or shopping in the same area is another factor that can draw customers to the franchise. Important factors to consider are as follows:

- The demographics of the market and surrounding area
- Ease of customer access to the location and easy access and exit.
- Proximity to competitors
- Noncompetitive attraction to the site
- Rental and site development costs relative to projected franchise cash flow and pro forma income statements
- Proposed future development adjacent to the proposed site, which could be positive or negative factors, such as new proposed commercial that could change traffic flow

To identify locations, the franchiser and franchisee should collaborate to maximize their results. Several site selection companies provide software that can be used by the franchiser to identify the best possible locations. Using the resources of a site selection company may be ob-tained at a reasonable cost, depending on how much responsibility the company assumes.

The franchise site selection process may extend to vendor purchasing programs. Quality site selection is advantageous to prospective vendors, while disjointed franchise locations may be an obstacle to the best vendor arrangement.

The Initial Franchise Fee and Continuing Payments

The Initial Franchise Fee and Continuing Payments refers to the financial resources that franchisees are obligated to transfer to the franchiser in exchange for franchise rights and support. Studies have shown there is a positive relationship between these types of fee, supporting the view that the initial franchise fee can enable the franchise system to build its brand and programs to support franchisees.[36] The initial franchise fee pays the franchiser for the rights to the trademark license, training, support, and the Franchise Operations Manual. Continuing fees are franchise royalty payments for ongoing rights to market products or services under the franchise brand, and to reimburse the franchiser for marketing and operational support. Continuing payments include contributions to an advertising fund for promotional and advertising programs on a local, regional, or national level. The average initial franchise fee for a franchise is $37,000, according to a study by Franchise Grade. The average franchise royalty rate was 6.8% in 2016, while average advertising fees increased to 2.5% in the same period.[37] Using agency theory, scholars have shown that continuing payments, specifically royalties, strengthen franchiser incentives to support franchises.[38] However, because continuing fees are a recurring operating expense, a franchiser should carefully examine whether these fees are competitive with comparable franchise systems, especially critical in the case of a startup. Franchisers employ various strategies to determine how royalty fees are calculated and structured. Royalty rates may vary, and franchisers use various methods for setting their royalty payments. Kona Ice, a successful franchiser, charges its franchisees a fixed royalty dollar amount which converts the royalty payment to a fixed expense. This approach differs from the traditional method where royalty dollars serve as a variable expense that rises when sales or profits increase. Some franchisers reduce royalty payments when a franchise reaches certain revenue tiers. Despite variations on how royalties are calculated and paid, most franchisers use the traditional method where royalties are calculated as a percentage of revenue.

The continuing fees paid by franchisees are the lifeblood of a franchise since these payments enable the franchiser to promote, support, and administer the franchise system. Still, it's important that continuing fees are equitable for both the franchisers and franchisees. Too few fees can prevent the franchiser from fulfilling its obligations to its franchisees. Continuing fees that are inequitable in terms of franchiser services and support can prevent franchisees from achieving their financial goals and result in dissatisfaction and poor system growth.

A part of continuing fees includes payments into an advertising fund that may be administered by the franchiser, or a committee of franchisers and franchisee representatives. Advertising funds are an effective way to leverage the collective financial and creative resources of franchises.

Franchise Term

Franchise Term refers to the length in years that a franchisee can run the franchise, which can range from 5 to 20 years. In addition to this initial term, most franchises have a renewal term of 5 years or more. This is important to franchisees who value a longer contract term since it provides more security. Favorable franchisee terms can be a competitive advantage and a longer franchise term can result in more earning power.

The average initial franchise term is 10.4 years and the average renewal term is 8.6 years.[39] A few franchisers will grant an initial franchise term without renewals. For example, McDonald's grants a 20-year franchise term with no renewals. The reasoning is based on the amount of the initial franchise investment and the expectation that knowing their franchise will terminate after 20 years, the franchisee will strive to maximize ROI. Given the success of McDonald's, it is hard to dismiss this policy, even though few others use this approach. In general, franchises that require a significant investment, such as hotel–motel franchises, grant longer terms than the typical franchise. Because the franchise term can be a factor in determining which franchise a prospective franchisee may choose, franchisers rarely differ when it comes to the franchise term.

Startup franchisers should exercise caution when establishing a franchise term lest they be considered an outlier. It is common for a startup to grant more favorable franchise terms to a first group of franchisees in order to be competitive. As the franchise system matures, the initial franchise fee and continuing fees paid by franchisees may increase.

Before the franchise term is due to expire, a franchisee must decide if they want to exercise their renewal option which requires the franchisee to provide the franchiser 6 months' notice, execute the current franchise agreement, remodel their franchise location to bring it up to current standards, and be in good standing under the terms of the franchise agreement. When a franchise does not exercise their renewal option, they risk losing the equity in their franchise since their options are to sell the franchise or allow the agreement to end.

Some franchisees choose to sell. In order to do so, they must meet certain conditions including approval of the franchiser and follow a procedure outlined in their franchise agreement. The terms that spell out how a franchise may be sold are relatively consistent among franchisers. They include the following:

- Supplying the franchiser 3 months' notice about their intent to sell the franchise.
- Sending the franchiser a franchise application and other pertinent information such as a letter of intent including terms of sale from the prospective buyer.
- The franchiser may have 60–90 days to approve the transaction. The franchiser retains right of first refusal which enables them to acquire the franchise for the same terms offered by the prospective buyer.

When franchise agreements approach the renewal stage, franchisees have three choices: renew their franchise agreement, sell their franchise or allow the agreement to expire, the least desirable option. When franchisers monitor franchisee satisfaction on a regular basis, there should be few surprises when franchise renewal time comes up. A healthy franchise system will encourage franchise renewals and establish an active franchise resale market, which is attractive to franchisee candidates when they establish an exit strategy.

Summary

This chapter presented key components of the franchise business model and provided definitions, explained their importance, and elaborated on key aspects. We started with the franchise IP and trademark which represent the foundation of all franchise systems. Using the examples of notable franchise brands, we explained the importance of the franchise operating system and why franchisers require franchisees to follow system standards. The importance of providing franchisees with the proper training before starting their new franchise operation is emphasized.

We continue our presentation of the fundamentals of franchising by illustrating the requirement that franchisers provide marketing, advertising, and ongoing support to enable franchisees to be successful. Vendor purchasing programs include a list of Approved Vendors, which requires franchisees to purchase certain products only from specific vendors. Approved vendor programs ensure that franchises use specific products that meet franchiser quality standards. Other important fundamentals include franchise territory, CI, the franchise term, fees, royalties, and contributions to advertising funds.

Notes

1 Bently, L., & Sherman, B. (2014). *Intellectual Property Law*. Oxford University Press, USA.

2 Autio, E., & Acs, Z. (2010). Intellectual property protection and the formation of entrepreneurial growth aspirations. *Strategic Entrepreneurship Journal, 4*(3), 234–251.

3 Windsperger, J., & Dant, R. P. (2006). Contractibility and ownership redirection in franchising: A property rights view. *Journal of Retailing, 82*(3), 259–272.

4 Terril, B., & Gotaskie, J. (2019). Protecting Intellectual Property Rights, Fox Rothchild LLP.
Rubin, P. H. (1978). The theory of the firm and the structure of the franchise contract. *The Journal of Law and Economics, 21*(1), 223–233.

5 Kelly, C., & Frantz, V. (2019). Franchisor's intellectual property and how to protect it. *IFA 52nd Annual Legal Symposium,*Washington, D.C.

6 Spinelli, S., & Birley, S. (1996). Toward a theory of conflict in the franchise system. *Journal of Business Venturing, 11*(5), 329–342. Michael, S. C. (1996). To franchise or not to franchise: An analysis of decision rights and organizational form shares. *Journal of Business Venturing, 11*(1), 57–71.

7 Norton, S. W. (1988). Franchising, brand name capital, and the entrepreneurial capacity problem. *Strategic Management Journal, 9*(S1), 105–114.

8 Zisk, R. (2019). *The Case for Effective Standard Enforcement.* International Franchise Association.
https://www.franchise.org/franchise-information/legal/case-effective-standards-enforcement

9 Falbe, C. M., & Welsh, D. H. (1998). NAFTA and franchising: A comparison of franchisor perceptions of characteristics associated with franchisee success and failure in Canada, Mexico, and the United States. *Journal of Business Venturing, 13*(2), 151–171.

10 Paswan, A. K., & Wittmann, C. M. (2009). Knowledge management and franchise systems. *Industrial Marketing Management, 38*(2), 173–180.

11 Justis, R. T., & Chan, P. S. (1991). Training for franchise management. *Journal of Small Business Management, 29*(3), 87.

12 Valerio, A., Parton, B., & Robb, A. (2014). *Entrepreneurship Education and Training Programs Around the World: Dimensions for Success.* The World Bank.

13 Frazer, L. (2001). Causes of disruption to franchise operations. *Journal of Business Research, 54*(3), 227–234.

14 Lusthaus, J. (2019). *What Should be Included in the Franchise Operations Manual,* Lusthaus Law Blog.
https://lusthausfranchiselaw.com/blog/what-should-be-included-in-the-franchise-operations-manual/

15 Dant, R. P., Grünhagen, M., & Windsperger, J. (2011). Franchising research frontiers for the twenty-first century. *Journal of Retailing, 87*(3), 253–268.

16 Sausaman, G. A. (2018). *Inside the Box: The Power of Complementary Branding.* Topper's Creamery (pp. 38–50).

17 Michael, S. C. (2002). Can a franchise chain coordinate? *Journal of Business Venturing, 17*(4), 325–341.

18 Ater, I., & Rigbi, O. (2015). Price control and advertising in franchising chains. *Strategic Management Journal, 36*(1), 148–158.

19 Brookes, M., & Altinay, L. (2011). Franchise partner selection: Perspectives of franchisors and franchisees. *Journal of Services Marketing, 25,* 336–348.

20 Watson, A. (2008). Small business growth through franchising: A qualitative investigation. *Journal of Marketing Channels, 15*(1), 3–21.

21 Watson, A., Dada, O. L., Grünhagen, M., & Wollan, M. L. (2016). When do franchisors select entrepreneurial franchisees? An organizational identity perspective. *Journal of Business Research*, 69(12), 5934–5945.

22 Knight, R. M. (1986). Franchising from the franchisor and franchisee points of view. *Journal of Small Business Management*, 24, 8–15.

23 Nyadzayo, M. W., Matanda, M. J., & Ewing, M. T. (2015). The impact of franchisor support, brand commitment, brand citizenship behavior, and franchisee experience on franchisee-perceived brand image. *Journal of Business Research*, 68(9), 1886–1894.

24 Seid, M. (2020). *What Support Can You Expect from the Franchisor*. MSA Worldwide Blog. https://www.msaworldwide.com/blog/what-support-can-you-expect-from-the-franchisor/#:~:text=Franchise%20systems%20are%20not%20fungible,factors%20unique%20to%20each%20franchise

25 Chiou, J. S., Hsieh, C. H., & Yang, C. H. (2004). The effect of franchisors' communication, service assistance, and competitive advantage on franchisees' intentions to remain in the franchise system. *Journal of Small Business Management*, 42(1), 19–36.

26 Michael, S. C. (2000). Investments to create bargaining power: The case of franchising. *Strategic Management Journal*, 21(4), 497–514.

27 Mazero, J., & Loonam, S. (2010). Purchasing cooperatives: Leveraging a supply chain for competitive advantage. *Franchise Law Journal*, 29, 148–163.

28 Loonan Triggs, S. (2010) *Purchasing Cooperatives: A Second Look*. Franchising.com

29 Butt, M. N., Antia, K. D., Murtha, B. R., & Kashyap, V. (2018). Clustering, knowledge sharing, and Interbrand competition: A multiyear analysis of an evolving franchise system. *Journal of Marketing*, 82(1), 74–92.

30 Mirmam, E. (2018). *You're Probably Keeping Tabs on Your Competitors All Wrong*. Entrepreneur.com. https://www.entrepreneur.com/article/310145

31 Goldstein, J. (2016). *Is your Franchise Territory Exclusive, Protected or non-Existant?* Goldstein Law Group.

32 Kalnins, A. (2004). An empirical analysis of territorial encroachment within franchised and company-owned branded chains. *Marketing Science*, 23(4), 476–489.

33 Yin, X., & Zajac, E. J. (2004). The strategy/governance structure fit relationship: Theory and evidence in franchising arrangements. *Strategic Management Journal*, 25(4), 365–383.

34 Park, K., & Khan, M. A. (2006). An exploratory study to identify the site selection factors for US franchise restaurants. *Journal of Foodservice Business Research*, 8(1), 97–114.

35 Chen, L. F., & Tsai, C. T. (2016). Data mining framework based on rough set theory to improve location selection decisions: A case study of a restaurant chain. *Tourism Management*, 53, 197–206.

36 Kaufmann, P. J., & Dant, R. P. (2001). The pricing of franchise rights. *Journal of Retailing*, 77(4), 537–545.

37 Franchise Grade (2017). *Facts and Figures, Historical Trends of Key Franchise Metrics*, July Issue.

38 Maruyama, M., & Yamashita, Y. (2012). Franchise fees and royalties: Theory and empirical results. *Review of Industrial Organization*, 40(3), 167–189.

39 Franchise Grade (2017). *Historical Trends of Key Franchise Metrics*.

Chapter 3

The Relevancy of Emerging Franchise Performance

After delineating the history, development, and fundamental components of the franchise business model, we will define emerging franchise
performance and illustrate the related data that pertains to emerging
franchise performance. On an annual basis, there are 300 or more new
franchise brands being launched in the United States and their performance, growth, and development vary dramatically. Like other types of
companies, the performance differences of franchise systems are often
shaped by industry-level factors.[1] A better understanding of franchise
performance differences would enable potential franchisors and franchisees to gain a greater understanding of emerging franchise performance. This can provide a clearer understanding of effective system
growth based upon the type of franchise products or services provided by
various franchise categories.

In the following section, we first discuss the nature of franchise performance and the corresponding performance measures. We then depict
the performance data and characteristics of emerging franchises which
are new franchise brands in their early growth stage.

Although the amount of franchise investment for emerging franchisors
is not related to franchise performance, we included the data because the
amount of investment has an impact on the number of franchise prospects an emerging franchisor can recruit.

Emerging Franchise Performance and Category Differences

Like capturing organizational performance,[2] franchise performance can
be conceptualized as the outcomes of a franchise system measured
against a particular set of goals or objectives. The evaluation can be how
an existing franchise system effectively executes its franchise program
financially, using specific measures of financial profitability, such as return on sales and return on assets.[3] It could also be broadly analyzed
with a mix of financial, product market, or non-financial indicators of

DOI: 10.4324/9781003034285-3

firm-level outcomes, such as sales growth, customer satisfaction, product/service quality, and market share.[4] According to a recent meta-analysis study,[5] different aspects of franchise performance have been found to be influenced by distinct sets of antecedents. For example, geographic dispersion is strongly associated with the proportion of outlets franchised and brand reputation while the outlet growth rate is associated with firm age and proportion of outlets franchised. Further, the number of new outlets is positively related to franchise size. These relationships often vary across different industries.

However, since emerging franchise systems are in various stages of growth with some having from 0 to 5 franchise locations, they lack the performance measures that established franchise brands have. As a result, the primary measure of emerging franchise performance is franchise system growth. Franchise system growth is one of the most significant measures of emerging franchise performance because positive franchise system growth is reflective of a healthy and vibrant franchise brand with features that attract qualified franchise candidates. An emerging franchise brand with strong growth has certain features that can attract and cause individuals to invest in the franchise.

Differentiating emerging franchise growth by specific attributes such as franchise category, franchisee investment, and how long it took emerging franchises to reach various growth stages is important for existing and potential franchisors. It can provide guidance on existing and future strategies based upon collective and specific emerging franchise performance. The performance of emerging franchises can provide an important indicator of whether entrepreneurs should utilize the franchise business model and can provide insight into the risk and potential success of implementing a franchising strategy.

Emerging Franchise Performance Data

Because of the systemic differences of emerging franchise performance across franchise categories, such as franchise locations, products, franchisee revenues, and required franchise investment, it is imperative for potential franchisors and franchisees to be aware of such differences and develop an in-depth knowledge of these variations. This knowledge will enable them to better understand the various benchmarks they can use to monitor the performance of their franchise systems. Franchise data are becoming more valuable because emerging franchisors will vie with mature franchises for qualified franchise candidates as it provides specific intelligence pertaining to the performance of their future competitors such as system growth, franchisee investment, franchise fees, size of franchise territories, and their outlet locations. With such information, potential franchisors may have a higher probability of success.

As Craig Tractenberg, franchise attorney with Fox Rothchild, states, emerging franchises' performance data are relevant and essential because it enables a business to measure and predict whether it is on course and will flourish. These data on emerging franchises debunk the preconceived notions of how franchise systems ought to grow and how to define success and what tends to work and what does not. Reviewing the data of opened and operating emerging franchise locations can help to predict how well the franchise program will thrive compared to company-operated units which deliver in real-time and provide feedback on customer preferences and product or service issues.

This knowledge can enable potential franchisors and franchisees to better gauge the likelihood on how they will plan their franchise strategy for a particular franchise category. For example, by better understanding the typical growth rates in a particular franchise category, they could better anticipate when growth would be expected and orchestrate the needed resources correspondingly.

For analysis and presentation, franchise brands are separated into franchise categories. The Entrepreneur 500, published by *Entrepreneur* Magazine, which ranks franchise brands based upon various criteria has published its Top 500 for 42 years. It ranks 100 different franchise categories. For example, one category is Childcare, Children's Enrichment programs, Children's Fitness, Children's Retail, and Tutoring.

The following analysis of franchise category growth in number of franchisees from 2010 to 2019 performed by Franchise Grade revealed that the top five franchise categories and their increase percent of growth were Property Management at 62%, Education, Entertainment, Sports Training at 53%, Pest Control at 51%, and Technology and Pharmacy at 48% (Figure 3.1).

This is essential information for potential franchisors who are considering launching a franchise in one of these categories or a related category because they've achieved strong growth for the past 5 years. Potential franchisors focused on a specific franchise category should first focus on the growth that category is achieving because it should demonstrate positive performance and a willingness for individuals to invest in that franchise category. Specific franchise data can be found in the Franchise Disclosure Document and franchise website. A franchise category that lacks growth may not be universally recognized nor an attractive franchise opportunity which can represent a major challenge for a new franchisor to attract franchisees and grow.

The importance of data and franchise category growth is exemplified by the history of the franchised frozen yogurt industry which was a popular franchise category several years ago exhibiting fast growth. This straightforward franchise concept had an advantage by being uncomplicated, however, it became a disadvantage because other franchise concepts chose

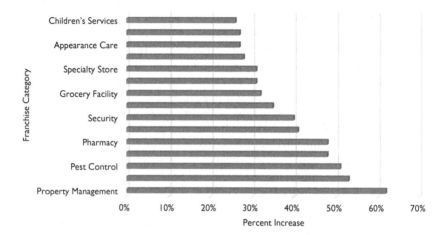

Figure 3.1 Top Category Growth from 2015 to 2019.

Note: Thompson, A. O. C. (2021). *Emerging Franchisee Data.* Franchise Grade.

to add frozen yogurt to their product line after witnessing the growth of yogurt franchises. This tactic by a number of fast-food franchise brands reduced the interest by franchise prospects in several yogurt franchise opportunities. There may be other examples of franchise concepts that can be easily replicated by an existing franchise brand. This possibility requires the potential franchisor to diligently analyze the performance and customer appeal of select fast growth franchise to determine whether they can sustain long-term growth or are a fad.

The Top Five Franchises in Five Franchise Categories

The following chart shows the top five franchises in five different franchise categories. This information can be used to compare and analyze those franchise brands that were leaders in their category. A potential franchisor can then refer to those franchised brands that most closely compares to the business that is being considered for franchising. As there are over 3,000 franchise brands, a reference such as the annual Entrepreneur 500 or Franchise Grade website can be referred to in order to identify specific franchise categories (Table 3.1).

Emerging Franchises System Growth

The rate of emerging franchise system growth refers to the growth and development of new and emerging franchises, which can have 0–100 franchise units. Emerging franchise data differs from franchise industry

Table 3.1 The Fastest Growing Franchise Categories from 2015 to 2020[6]

Fitness and Gyms	Children's Services	Wellness/Nutrition	Ethnic	Coffee and Bakery
Orange Theory Fitness	Code Ninjas	Massage Envy Spa	Hissho, Oumi Sushi	Kung Fu Tea
Club Pilates	Best Brains	Seva Beauty	Sushibox	Bambu Desserts & Drinks
F45 Training	Urban Air Trampoline & Adventure Park	OsteoStrong	BonChon	Vitality Bowls
ilovekickboxing.com	Apex Fun Run	The camp Transformation Center	The Halal Guys	Ben's Soft Pretzels
Gracie Barra	British Swim School	Stretch Zone	Taziki's Mediterranean Café	La Madeleine Country French Cafe

data, which includes all franchises regardless of age or system size while emerging franchises could include startup franchise brands without any franchisees. For the potential franchisor, emerging franchise performance data are important because it provides information on how long it took for those franchises to reach a certain system size. This statistic can be used to identify the effectiveness of those emerging franchisors to recruit and sell franchises. When a new franchise brand has growth, it indicates that individuals are attracted to that business concept. In addition to generating franchise fees and royalties, each new franchisee helps to create interest in the franchise and instill confidence on the part of the franchisor employees and its existing franchisees.

When considering franchising an existing business, the data on the growth of emerging franchise systems across categories can be helpful for the decision-making process. To identify system growth for a category of franchise brands, such as home care franchises, an analysis of those franchises can be done by analyzing the websites and FDDs of several home care franchises that have been in operation for a minimum of 5 years. The other option is to utilize the services of a franchise consulting or market research firm.

Some franchise categories can be difficult to compete with like franchise brands which have multiunit operated franchisees. Lodging and auto service franchises comprise 40%–50% of the entire lodging and automotive service revenues. For example, lodging franchises such as Hilton, Holiday Inns, Hotel 6, and Days Inn and automotive franchises such as AAMCO, Meineke, Midas, and Jiffy Lube when combined with independents would represent formidable competitors for potential franchisors who may be considering launching a franchise in these categories. The appropriate franchise intelligence into these franchise categories could prevent a potential franchisor from failure by competing against highly competitive franchise brands.[7]

Poor franchise growth can negatively influence the ability to attract new franchisees, cause a drain on franchisor capital, and can create apprehension on the part of potential franchisees. Some franchise candidates are apprehensive about investing in a franchise system with few franchisees coupled with slow system growth. A frequent question on the part of franchise candidates is how long has the franchise been in operation and how many franchises are there? The type of response to this question can determine whether a candidate will continue to pursue that franchise or seek a different franchise opportunity.

Emerging franchises grow at various stages, with some franchises growing at a faster rate, with others growing slowly or not at all. As First Author, I was an executive with several emerging franchise brands and when we wrote our business plan, we established our franchise development goals to begin 3 months after launching the new franchise program. For the first full year of operations, we set 3–5 franchise sales, and for the second full year 6–8 franchise sales as the goal.

When there are few or no comparable franchise businesses, potential franchisors could enjoy the first-mover advantage. However, this situation can be a disadvantage because they would have to demonstrate to franchisee candidates the benefit and potential of their franchise system and business model. Educating potential franchises in such an environment could be quite costly, making it time-consuming to grow a franchise system in such a unique franchise business. Thus, the fact that most businesses of a particular industry have not been franchised should be an important warning sign for a potential franchisor.

The following statistics from a recent Franchise Grade study of Emerging franchises from 2010 to 2020 reveals the potential and the consequences of launching an emerging franchise program:

A 10-year review of over 1,119 Emerging franchises from 2010 to 2020 showed that the top five categories were represented by franchises that provided services such as home care, children's educational services, and beauty and hair grooming which represented 34% (Figure 3.2). The next highest percent at 21% consisted of fast-food franchises including chicken, hamburgers, sandwiches, coffee, and breakfast franchises. These results are pertinent for potential franchisors because they provide emerging franchise performance for various franchise categories.

The analysis also found that of those that started four years prior, 27.4% had 0–1 franchise locations, 50% that operated for ten years had 50 or fewer franchise locations and 15.6% of the franchises reached

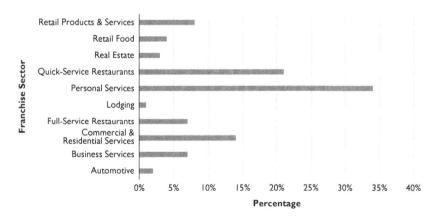

Figure 3.2 10-Year Review of Over 1,119 Emerging Franchises from 2010 to 2020.

Note: *Analysis of Emerging Franchises* (2021). FranchiseGrade. file:///C:/Users/carol%20eddie/Documents/analysis-emerging-franchises_3.pdf

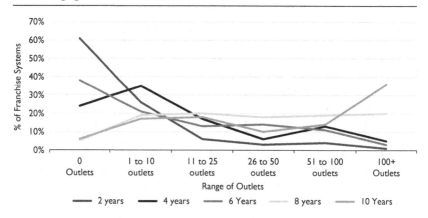

Figure 3.3 Emerging Franchise Growth from 2010 to 2020.

Note: *Analysis of Emerging Franchises* (2021). FranchiseGrade. file:///C:/Users/carol%20eddie/ Documents/analysis-emerging-franchises_3.pdf

100+ locations after 6–8 years of franchising (Figure 3.3).[8] The number of franchises that reached or surpassed 100 locations represents a significant accomplishment for those brands. As the average number of franchise locations added was 50, the emerging franchise brands that achieved this level of growth possessed certain characteristics or features that made them desirable franchise investments.

Amount of Franchise Investment

Although not a specific measure of emerging franchise performance the amount of franchisee investment plays a key role in emerging franchise growth. Franchise investment is defined as the amount of money an individual must invest in a franchise. The lower the franchise investment the larger the number of potential franchise prospects a franchisor can draw from. Depending upon the franchise sector and category, the initial investment can range from less than $50,000 for a home-based service franchise to over several million for a restaurant or motel franchise.

When the investment for a new franchise is higher compared to comparable franchise brands it can retard new franchise growth. Potential franchisees will scrutinize the new franchise opportunity even more because the emerging franchisor will lack any franchise performance history so it must rely upon successful company operations for validation. This is an important reason why the emerging franchisor should be able to demonstrate strong leadership and a successful track record in the performance of its core business. When a potential franchisor designs the structure of their new franchise program it is important that they consider the amount of the required franchisee investment by recognizing that the higher the investment the smaller the number of potential franchisees. The lowest franchise investments tend to occupy the service categories such as home care, children's services, and residential and commercial services while the highest franchise investments are found in the food, lodging categories, and large retail categories.

As franchise investors are concerned about the degree of risk when considering a franchise opportunity, a high franchisee investment for a new franchise will invite increased due diligence by a prospective franchisee. Emerging franchises that require a high investment must have strong appeal, impressive market potential, and favorable prospects for an attractive franchisee financial return.

In a study conducted by Franchise Grade, 41.6% of emerging franchise brands had an average franchise investment under $250,000. In the group, 28% of the emerging franchises had an average investment in the $100,000–$250,000 range. There were 14% of emerging franchises in the study that required an investment under $100,000. These results reflect the popularity of personal services, commercial and residential home services, and home-based franchises which have lower investment requirements.

A company considering franchising their business model should have a comprehensive 5-year business plan including franchise sector analytics and a competitive overview. They should gather and compile franchise performance data pertaining to the franchise sector and category that pertains to their business model. Consideration should be given to the potential appeal of the franchise products or services to prospective franchisees and consumers. The plan should identify and project realistic franchise unit economics which are used by franchisors to identify or project the profitability of a franchise at the unit level. The reason certain emerging franchise sectors are more successful than others is due in great part to consumer demand for their products and services. As a result, entrepreneurs considering franchising as a growth strategy should be aware of the composition of similar and successful franchises both emerging and established.

Summary

In this chapter, we presented data that revealed how companies and entrepreneurs that implemented the franchise business model can experience various rates of growth. We demonstrated why potential franchisors should be aware of emerging franchise performance by presenting franchise category data that identify franchise categories that had the highest sustained growth. Potential franchisors should compare their proposed franchise concept to comparable franchise categories to identify how well they have performed. We discussed how emerging franchises grow and the fact that an emerging franchise can experience slow growth that could cause them to leave franchising altogether. The importance of growth for an emerging system was demonstrated by presenting historical data that showed which emerging franchise categories grew faster than others. Also, we explained the reasons why certain emerging franchises succeed while others may struggle or fail.

We indicated how the size of the initial franchisee investment can affect the ability to attract franchise prospects and a high franchisee investment can attract fewer prospects. Franchise performance data for emerging franchises is a key component of the potential franchisor's tool kit when designing and constructing their new franchise business.

Notes

1 Chan, C. S. R., Patel, P. C., & Phan, P. H. (2020). Do differences among accelerators explain differences in the performance of member ventures? Evidence from 117 accelerators in 22 countries. *Strategic Entrepreneurship Journal, 14*(2), 224–239. McGahan, A. M., & Porter, M. E. (1997). How much does industry matter, really? *Strategic Management Journal, 18*(S1), 15–30. Short, J. C., Ketchen Jr., D. J., Palmer, T. B., & Hult, G. T. M. (2007). Firm, strategic group, and industry influences on performance. *Strategic Management Journal, 28*(2), 147–167. Patel, P. C., & Chan, C. R. (2021). Non-economic performance of benefit corporations: A variance decomposition approach. *Journal of Business Ethics*, 1–22.
2 Richard, P. J., Devinney, T. M., Yip, G. S., & Johnson, G. (2009). Measuring organizational performance: Towards methodological best practice. *Journal of Management, 35*(3), 718–804.
3 Barthélemy, J. (2008). Opportunism, knowledge, and the performance of franchise chains. *Strategic Management Journal, 29*(13), 1451–1463.
4 Wu, C. W. (2015). Antecedents of franchise strategy and performance. *Journal of Business Research, 68*(7), 1581–1588.
5 Kang, J., Asare, A. K., Brashear-Alejandro, T., & Li, P. (2018). Drivers of franchisor growth: A meta-analysis. *Journal of Business & Industrial Marketing, 33*(2), 196–207.
6 Thompson, A. O. C. (2021). *Emerging Franchisee Data*. Franchise Grade.
7 Usher, J. M. (1999). Specialists, generalists, and polymorphs: spatial advantages of multiunit organization in a single industry. *Academy of Management Review, 24*(1), 143–150.
8 Franchise Grade. *2021 Emerging Franchise Report*. https://www.franchisegrade.com/reports/download/analysis-emerging-franchises_3/start

Chapter 4

Evaluating the Franchise Venture

Chapter 3 presented statistics and commentary on how emerging franchises perform differently across major industries. These performance differences illustrate the emerging trend of franchise growth and highlight the importance of attending to industry-level factors that could shape the success and failure of franchise programs. Potential franchisors and franchisees could use franchise performance information to gauge potential growth and possible obstacles that they may encountered when operating in a particular industry.

Chapter 4 discusses the next step in the franchising process, the evaluation of the franchise venture. It is essential for franchisors to carefully examine their qualifications for adopting a franchising strategy. Studies have indicated that business planning significantly improved new venture performance.[1] While the planning–performance relationship seems weaker for new ventures,[2] franchisors should still carefully examine franchising strategies before implementing them, to avoid jeopardizing their financial health, sharpen their potential franchise business models, and improve their overall chance of profitability.

In the following sections, we define the evaluation process and illustrate its importance. We demonstrate an initial thought experiment for potential franchisors and franchisees in order to quickly examine the feasibility of a franchise strategy. We then describe the five major aspects of a recommended evaluation process. We begin by examining the company's growth objectives and elaborate on four additional criteria: Company Credentials, Business Qualifications for Franchising, Franchisee Return on Investment, and Pausing the Franchise Program. Carefully examined, these aspects may help potential franchisors determine the probability of success by implementing a franchise strategy.

The Evaluation Process and Its Importance

This process illustrates extensive procedures to determine whether an existing or proposed business has the attributes necessary to become a

DOI: 10.4324/9781003034285-4

successful franchise system. This process involves careful examination of essential internal and external factors. The objective is to compare the present values of a company developing its own business units versus franchising the business for others to expand into unexplored regions. This will help to identify the probability of success or failure and whether a franchise venture should continue. If the results of this analysis are positive, the next step would be to build a franchise system by carefully documenting various aspects of business operations.

According to the business planning literature,[3] failure to conduct this process could jeopardize the financial health of an existing business and its franchise units. Building and launching a franchise program can require a substantial outlay of capital for legal services, consulting, marketing, franchisee recruitment, and staff. Because it can take time for initial franchise fees and royalty income from franchisees to become available to enhance company operations, initial capital is critical. Certain franchise sectors, such as lodging and food concepts, require a higher capital investment because of the higher costs of creating operation manuals, franchise design and decor, purchasing equipment, securing site locations, and remodeling stores, compared to service franchises. Because franchising an existing business can represent a substantial investment for a small business, failing to thoroughly analyze whether the business has enough capital for the project might lead to poor financial management and premature failure of adopting franchising strategy.

An evaluation process can help potential franchisors not only to avoid making the wrong decision but sharpen aspects of their business model. If the focus and emphasis are on the franchise concept, company deficiencies may be overlooked, which can jeopardize the launch and success of a franchise program. Some companies are so confident of their new franchise venture they overlook key aspects of their business. One startup franchisor with an in-the-home maintenance business for seniors who did not properly test his concept or analyze his potential market ended up closing his business. Another franchisor spent the bulk of his investment capital on a poorly qualified consultant, under whose guidance he franchised before thoroughly qualifying his company. He ended up with only one franchise and a franchise system that failed to take off.

These companies failed because they did not fully qualify their companies before franchising. By following a franchise evaluation process, there is less risk in overlooking an important area. While this evaluation process could and should be time-consuming, potential franchisors should conduct the thought experiment below to gauge whether a franchising strategy would be appropriate and effective for them.

Initial Thought Experiment

Before devoting a significant amount of resources to evaluate franchising as a potential growth strategy, people should conduct a simple initial thought experiment, comparing Starbucks Coffee Company and Subway's franchise growth strategies to envision how these could align with their business and personal preferences.[4] This experiment involves juxtaposing Starbucks' company-operated and licensing program with Subway's franchise program, one that reveals major differences between a large chain operated by franchisees compared to a large chain of company-operated locations.

Although both companies sought to increase their revenue by adding new retail stores, Starbucks used company-operated locations and incentivized managers through training and stock options to gain employee buy-in and commitment, while Subway utilized franchising to make sure managers had ownership and equity in their own business in order to gain brand loyalty. Companies that provide certain consumer food products have found that franchising is a more effective business model when the objective is to expand to a national chain. Examples of this strategy include Dunkin', Chick-fil-A, Pizza Hut, and Taco Bell.

Retail chains that provide durable goods and clothing have not embraced the franchise model for expansion, due to the need for strong control over pricing and marketing strategies. For a company as big as Starbucks to successfully operate a large national chain is a unique outcome. The comparison between Subway and Starbucks may prompt entrepreneurs to recognize the advantages and disadvantages of the franchise model and help them better estimate whether such strategy could align with their business. This experiment, however, only focuses on whether to franchise or develop company locations. To proceed, we recommend the potential franchisors carefully examine the growth objectives of their company and consider if these objectives could align with a franchising strategy.

Confirming Company Objectives

Perhaps, the most important aspect of the franchise evaluation process is the careful examination of company objectives. Potential franchisors should ensure that company performance objectives are closely aligned with franchising strategy. Doing so will not only set a performance benchmark for potential franchisors to systematically compare franchising to other growth strategies but help them to plan and orchestrate their resources to achieve these objectives.

Different company objectives reflect different growth vehicles that require different sets of resources and strategies for entrepreneurs to grow their companies. In addition to franchise strategy, another frequently utilized strategy is the expansion of company-owned units in different locations. Next, we compare the advantages and disadvantages of the franchise and company growth strategy based on company resources and objectives.

One goal that potential franchisors incorporate to determine company growth objectives is the size of business units. While some franchisors seek to add 3–5 franchise units during the first 3 years, others develop a more aggressive growth objective by setting a goal of 20 new franchise locations per year.

If fast growth of the business locations is the primary growth objective, franchising offers the best method to achieve that goal. Unlike the case where a franchisee funds the investment in a new location, a company location must be funded by the company. This approach may require as much capital investment for one company location as the cost to launch an entire franchise program. The deciding factor is whether the growth of locations is the primary objective.

a   In order to achieve fast franchise system growth, the franchisor will need to offer potential franchisees the opportunity to acquire multi-unit franchisee rights, which requires the development of numerous unit locations over a set period of say, 2–5 years, versus unit franchise growth which grants the rights to one franchise location.

b   If retaining company revenues and earnings are more important than fast growth, a company growth strategy will make sense compared to franchisees retaining profits after paying an initial franchise fee and a small percentage of revenues in royalties to the franchisor.

c   If the company is not able to find enough qualified franchisees, it may have difficulty benefiting from the franchise process. Some companies avoid franchising because they fear potential lawsuits from disgruntled franchisees.

d   Smaller companies seeking to expand may prefer the franchise model because they lack the financial and human resources to launch company-owned locations.

e   Control is an important consideration for some businesses. Certain retail businesses exercise a high degree of control over product and promotional pricing. This is the reason why many clothing, supermarket, and other retail businesses don't franchise.

f   Managing company locations is costly and labor-intensive compared to a franchise model, where the franchisee manages the day-to-day operation, is highly motivated, and is financially vested in the franchise.

g   Market expansion strategy is an important factor because franchise locations can be established in different markets at the same time, compared to adding one location at a time.

h   Company leadership may have financial and business reasons to limit investing in company locations and prefer implementing the franchise model.

The advantages and disadvantages between two main growth strategies, franchising, and company-owned locations, require potential franchisors to carefully examine the alignment between their company objectives and a particular franchising strategy. Once this alignment has been confirmed, potential franchisors may move on to evaluate their own competence and qualifications for using a franchise business model to grow and develop a business.

Five Key Aspects of the Evaluation Process

After ensuring alignment between company growth objectives and franchising strategy, potential franchisors can move on to the evaluation process. This consists of five major activities that may be done sequentially or concurrently. Potential franchisors may rotate these activities if desired, as they may trigger useful ideas and insights on other aspects of the evaluation process. We discuss five aspects of franchise evaluation: Internal Feasibility Analysis – Resource Availability, Internal Feasibility Analysis – Franchisability of the Core Business, External Feasibility Analysis – Industry Practice and Trend, Franchisee Return on Investment (ROI), and Final Check.

Internal Feasibility Analysis – Resource Availability

The first aspect of the evaluation process is conducting an internal feasibility analysis. In order to review the likelihood of a company successfully creating, launching, and executing a franchise program, potential franchisors must conduct a careful examination of various capabilities of the company and determine whether there are sufficient and/or unique resources to design and implement a corresponding franchising strategy.[5] This does not mean that potential franchisors need to possess significant capabilities to start their franchise program. Next, we elaborate on two major categories of company capabilities that should be closely examined: financial capital and management/employee competence.

Financial Capital

Financial capital is essential in order for firms to plan, execute, and develop a franchising strategy. Estimated initial investment in a new franchise program may range from $100,000 to $500,000, depending on the size of the operation and corresponding industry. The company should have ample capital to build, staff, and launch the franchise program. If it does not, it will have difficulty funding a franchise venture, building a profitable franchise model, or neglecting operational or marketing areas. This will jeopardize the success of the entire project. Indeed, many emerging franchisors have foundered and eventually failed because the company lacked the capital to fund and develop a franchise project.

If the franchise project is considered a viable venture, a company that lacks suitable funding may seek capital from external investors such as family members, friends, or angel investors. However, equity investors such as private equity groups and venture capitalists may have little interest in a franchise startup unless they can extract an extraordinary return on their investment.

An initial investment must be backed by a history of profitable company financial performance that provides a continuous stream of financial resources to help potential franchisors build and develop their franchise operation. It can also demonstrate the feasibility and application of company operations to convince potential franchisees to adopt and duplicate the existing business model. The importance of a firm profitability history is echoed by numerous experts. According to Steve Begleman, CEO of SMB Franchise Advisors, "the company or pilot operation should have a positive sales trend and sustained profitability. Without a positive sales trend and good earnings history, the company is not prepared to franchise. When a company cannot demonstrate a history of continuing sales growth, then the due diligence performed by a prospective franchisee will reveal this flaw and deter them from wanting to invest in the new franchise."

Management/Employee Competence

The management competence of the top management team is the second key aspect of company abilities that should be carefully examined for an internal feasibility analysis. The leadership and stability of a company is a critical factor in deciding whether to implement the franchise business model. A strong management team should represent the franchisor. The leader of the company needs to possess the traits required to build and launch a new business. Starting a franchise results in the operation of two companies: the current business and the new franchise. When a company lacks the necessary leadership to oversee the operation of both the existing company and new franchise operation, it may face difficulties.

The executive leader should have the proven business skills and experience that implementation of a new entity requires. This includes experience starting a new business, the ability to identify the skills required by supporting staff, and proven skills in business operations, finance, and marketing. In essence, they must be a well-rounded businessperson.

A potential franchisor leader should possess traits common to successful franchisor founders and leaders.

- Be a visionary, who see a realistic path to building a successful franchise system.
- Has a plan and strategy for growth, based on sound principles and realistic. expectations. Some potential franchisors imagine future system growth as if they are the next McDonald's.
- Recognize the importance of franchisees earning a reasonable profit and return on their investment.
- See the importance of obtaining franchisee feedback when appropriate, and gain franchisee buy-in before making significant changes to franchise products and major promotional programs.
- The existing company should be successful business operation.

In addition, the management team should be knowledgeable in technological and business aspects that are essential to the core business of a franchise system. Knowledge areas are important because such a base allows the top management team to create a comprehensive operating manual that can facilitate the transfer of essential knowledge to potential franchisees. It may help them to resolve potential operating issues that franchisees could encounter. This knowledge base enables the top management team to develop training programs to pass down important skill sets relevant to the franchise business.

Vehicle Tracking Solutions (VTS) located in Deer Park, New York, was a growing company that provided automatic vehicle location products, enabling its customers to see the location of a vehicle and other data, on terminals that use a proprietary software program. After careful analysis, John Cunningham, the CEO, decided in 2007 to implement a franchise program for VTS expansion, which was achieving strong growth. Some of the newly recruited franchisees experienced problems, due in part to their lack of technical knowledge and weak business-to-business selling skills. It proved difficult for corporate headquarters to provide technical support for VTS products thousands of miles away, which resulted in dissatisfied franchisees and customers.

After careful consideration, Cunningham decided amicably terminate the franchise agreements. Today, VTS flourishes as a highly successful fleet tracking company because its leadership and stability allowed it to make a dramatic shift to its growth strategy. For certain companies, especially those with unique operating systems, success may be easier to achieve when the company maintains full control over its operation.

In addition to management capability, a potential franchisor should evaluate the capabilities of current company staff to determine whether they can effectively work in the new franchise company. Good interpersonal communication and selling skills are needed to interact with franchise candidates. They also need to counsel and advise franchisees, recognizing that the franchisee is not an employee. In some cases, this can require a degree of diplomacy. Evaluating whether an individual possesses these traits should be based on their performance as a company employee such as how they interact with subordinates and colleagues.

Internal Feasibility Analysis – Franchisability of the Core Company Attributes

The second aspect of the evaluation process is examining key company attributes to determine the franchisability of the core business model, such as whether the business used to build the franchise has the attributes to qualify as a successful franchise. It is important to gather preliminary data and information on the existing business operations to determine whether its core business model can be easily implemented in different locations facing various competitors and consumers. Doing so will help benchmark key metrics against comparable franchise systems.

The first company attribute is brand equity. This refers to the social value of a company/product brand name and is a key factor in shaping a company's revenue, as the products of well-recognized brands are generally perceived to be better than those of lesser-known brands.[6] Although recently launched franchise systems may not be well recognized at the national level, potential franchisees could still evaluate company performance and reputation in local markets as a heuristic to determine franchisability. This suggests that potential franchisors need to carefully manage and build their brand equity.

For example, they should make sure the company trademark has been registered, and if not, the company should have a trademark search completed and the mark registered. The franchise trademarks represent the foundation of a franchise system. Without a protected trademark, the value of the franchise may be diminished and competitors could infringe on the trademark. It's not unusual for a company to try to save money using an online legal service to register a trademark, not always the best decision, since the service may not include a comprehensive trademark search. Most online legal services companies provide a minimal number of services at a low cost. As additional services cost more, for someone not familiar with various aspects of trademark law, this can be a problem.

The second attribute to be examined is the number of company-owned units operating across various locations. Emerging franchise systems that are launched by a company with multiple company-owned units usually perform better than franchises launched from a company with a single unit. Multiple company operations provide competitive advantages for a startup franchise program because such experience enables potential franchisors and top management to acquire valuable knowledge, skills, and abilities that will help in the duplication, modifications, and implementations of the core business model in new locations.[7] Such experience will help franchisors deal with competitors and customers at various locations. Multiple company locations can provide additional revenue streams to fund the operation and marketing of franchising strategies, further strengthening bargaining power with existing vendors to obtain purchasing benefits. Finally, multiple company operations often impress potential franchisees and lead to more favorable evaluations of the franchise system.

The third attribute is the repeat customer rate, a simple ratio of the number of return customers to the total number of customers. The business a potential franchisor operates should differ from popular restaurant that attracts loyal diners and rely heavily on repeat customers. A heavy reliance on repeat customers suggests that franchising may not be optimal because this type of businesses, commonly observed in legal and financial services, advertising, or public relations, may be difficult to replicate and export to new markets. Such businesses often rely upon a personal and enduring relationship between service providers and their clients. Such a relationship is difficult to replicate in a franchise model which is based on the ability to systemize a business concept. When a business is based on a personal relationship rather than a business model, such a franchise model is not easily replicable.

The fourth attribute is the marketing plan of the existing business. This should be a unique selling plan that makes the business attractive in terms of market appeal.[8] A proposed franchise should have such features as a product with certain unique features, a market that will allow potential customers to want to use products, and the ability to compete against similar franchises and independent businesses that may offer similar products. If a franchise doesn't have these features, it may be difficult to find qualified prospects willing to invest in the franchise.

The fifth attribute to consider is whether there are existing guidelines or manuals that document the business operation. Such documents provide potential franchisors with the materials to duplicate the core business model.[9] It can determine how easily an existing business may be duplicated by examining whether there are easily teachable procedures. If such documentation is not available, it should be created quickly. If, however, after careful evaluation potential franchisors cannot come up with a standardized operation of the core business, this is a signal that the franchise operation cannot easily be replicated or taught, and that such companies should not move forward in adopting a franchising strategy.

External Feasibility Analysis – Industry Practices and Trends

An important aspect of the evaluation process is to conduct an external feasibility analysis by examining whether there are existing franchising systems offering similar products/services within the same industry, in particular, whether a franchise category exists in a targeted industry. Potential franchisors utilize such resources as the Entrepreneur 500 Ranking Report which contains over 100 franchise categories, or Franchisegrade.com, which allows users to filter a choice of various franchise categories and make comparisons among key franchise attributes such as fees, number of locations, and estimated franchisee investment.

If a franchise category already exists, it is important to identify the industry trend by examining how well such franchise systems are performing. For example, certain franchise concepts such as fitness, childcare, senior care, and certain food concepts are popular franchise categories, i.e., acceptable to consumers in most consumer markets. Other franchise products or services may be more appropriate for certain markets and geographic areas, such as high-end sit-down restaurants or franchises that feature ethnic foods. In these cases, the marketing strategy needs to be targeted and carefully researched, which may mean focusing on markets with higher-income residents, located in major metropolitan areas or an appropriate ethnic population, such as Miami, New York City, or Los Angeles. When there is concern about marketability, it's important to engage the services of a market research firm to perform an in-depth analysis before investing substantial capital into a franchise.

A company that is considering franchising in a competitive category dominated by several popular franchise systems should be diligent when it comes to evaluating any potential difficulty competing against dominant franchise brands. Without unique features, an emerging franchise may have problems facing an existing brand that can compete from a position of strength. For example, franchising a chicken concept may mean competing with a formidable franchise brand and strong market share. Starting a new franchise system in such a competitive category can sometimes be an advantage, as competitiveness can reflect increasing consumer demand. The growth of home care franchise brands has resulted in the lack of attractive franchise territories. Because of the demand for home care services, this may be seen as an opportunity for new home care franchise brands in those territories. Conversely, some franchise brands are so dominant (such as McDonald's or Chick-Fil-A), a franchise startup could find it difficult to penetrate that market area. Key decision factors are the size of the market, potential customer demand, and number of competing locations.

On the other hand, if the franchise is a new concept without competition from existing franchise systems, this may be an advantage or disadvantage, depending upon certain factors and whether similar franchises preceded the potential franchise program.

- A potential franchisor should identify similar franchise brands and find out if some have been successful or failed, and how they performed.
- Lack of existing franchise competition could be a warning sign of low customer demand for the franchise products or services. This may require a marketing study.
- A competitive analysis that reveals few if any franchise competitors may mean the potential franchisor could have an advantage, providing there is ample demand for the products or services. An example is home care franchises which 15 years ago had only five franchise brands but now boast 70. The growth in this sector is the result of a reasonable franchise investment in the $100,000–125, 000 range, coupled with strong market demand for home care services, driven by an aging population.
- Lack of a competitive franchise climate may be a disadvantage when a business is difficult to replicate. Evaluating whether a business has such attributes can answer the question of whether lack of existing franchise competitors is a disadvantage.

Franchisee Profitability, Cash Flow, and Return on Investment

The last aspect of the evaluation process is to analyze expected profitability, cash flow, and return on investment (ROI) for potential franchisees. This is important, as it enables franchisors to evaluate the likelihood of attracting enough franchisees to grow a profitable franchise system.

When potential franchisees consider investing in a franchise, they want to identify potential earnings, or if not, feel confident that they can achieve those earnings. Otherwise, they will not be willing to invest in the franchise. Related to projected earnings is the cash flow a franchise will generate. It's expected that at the start of a franchise operation there will be some negative cash flow, which will turn positive within a reasonable period of time, for example, 6 months. To project franchise earnings and cash flow, i.e., how much ROI they can expect from their franchise investment, may be difficult. Given potential ROI may vary across different franchise systems and industries, potential franchisors need to carefully identify potential earnings and cash flow and ROI to determine whether they can successfully franchise their core business.

To identify potential earnings, cash flow, and ROI, potential franchisors should prepare a pro forma income statement, cash flow projection, and estimated ROI. A pro forma income statement should include projected revenues, gross margin, operating expenses, royalties, and continuing fees projecting pretax income.

A pro forma income statement and cash flow projection should depict several financial models to establish potential breakeven and income points for the franchise operation. Pro forma income statements and cash flow projections are critical to the introduction of an emerging franchise program. Without this information, the company can't confirm if it's feasible to franchise. If a company doesn't do financial projections but overlays franchise fees onto an existing company income statement, it may result in an inaccurate depiction of projected franchise income. This could distort the required investment and breakeven points.

It is critical that the emerging franchise program is built on accurate and realistic financial information. When projected franchise financial performance is based upon unrealistic expectations or inaccurate financial data, a new franchisee may face the possibility of failure. Companies and entrepreneurs looking to launch a franchise program can act in haste and focus more effort on the operational and marketing components of the franchise versus establishing credible financial estimations. Because franchisees invest their own capital in a franchise, it is critical to estimate potential ROI and understand its components while evaluating the feasibility of a franchise system. Estimated ROI should be based on realistic and reasonable expectations so that potential franchisors can move on and devote resources to planning and implementing their franchising strategy.

In terms of estimated franchisee ROI, it is generally accepted in the franchise industry that the pretax income of a franchise operation should range from 30% to 50% of the total franchisee investment. This would include additional income in return for investment, time, and effort expended in operating the new franchise location. In many cases, a franchisee will draw a weekly or monthly salary, so pretax income would be lower, due to this added expense and result in an ROI of 15%–20%.

Whether the company has one location or ten, it is critical to incorporate existing company financial statements into the creation of a pro forma income statement. After adding proposed royalty fees and other franchise operating expenses to the proposed franchise model, it should be possible to show examples of projected potential franchise earnings. Calculations used to compute franchise royalties and other fees should be drawn from competitive franchise systems or inputting franchise fees into the financial model. Franchise projections should be realistic, based on existing company performance and reasonable expectations of a franchisee-led operation (Figure 4.1).

PROFORMA INCOME STATEMENT AND CASH FLOW PROJECTION

MONTH	1	2	3	4	5	6	7	8	9	10	11	12	TOTAL
CASH ON HAND	1,00,000	71,455	69,135	61,675	59,670	60,022	60,752	60,062	62,177	64,497	61,097	68,037	71,512
SALES	0	20,000	25,000	30,000	35,000	40,000	40,000	50,000	50,000	55,000	60,000	60,000	4,65,000
GM DOLLARS	0	6,000	7,500	9,000	10,500	12,000	12,000	15,000	15,000	16,500	18,000	18,000	1,39,500
TOTAL CASH	1,00,000	77,455	78,135	70,675	70,170	72,022	72,752	75,062	71,177	80,997	79,097	86,027	9,33,569
EXPENSES													
Rent	1,000	1,000	1,000	1,000	1,000	1,000	1,000	1,000	1,000	1,000	1,000	1,000	12,000
Salaries	4,000	4,000	4,000	5,000	5,000	6,000	6,000	6,500	6,500	7,000	7,000	7,500	68,500
Telephone	500	500	500	600	600	600	700	700	700	700	700	700	7,500
Advertising	3,000	1,000	1,500	1,500	1,500	1,500	2,000	2,000	2,000	2,000	2,000	2,000	22,000
Office Supplies	1,000	250	250	0	0	250	0	0	350	0	0	350	2,450
Equipment	10,000	0	0	0	0	0	0	0	0	0	0	0	10,000
Travel&Entertainment	2,000	250	250	250	250	250	250	250	250	250	250	250	4,750
Leases	300	300	300	300	300	300	300	300	300	300	300	300	3,600
Insurance	625	0	0	625	0	0	0	625	0	0	0	625	2,500
Deposits	3,000	0	0	0	0	0	0	0	0	0	0	0	3,000
Professional Fees	2,000	0	0	0	0	0	500	0	0	500	0	0	3,000
Utilities	500	0	0	500	0	0	500	0	0	500	0	0	2,000
Postage	120	120	120	120	120	120	120	120	120	120	120	120	1,440
Misc.	500	200	200	200	200	200	200	200	200	200	200	200	2,700
Royalty 5%	0	1000	1250	1500	1750	2000	2000	2500	2500	2750	3000	3000	23,250
Ad Fund 2%	0	400	500	600	700	800	800	1000	1000	1100	1200	1200	9,300
Total Expenses	28,545	9,020	9,870	12,195	11,420	13,020	14,370	15,195	14,920	16,420	15,770	17,245	1,77,990
Pre-Tax Income	28,545	2,320	1,960	2,005	590	730	690	2,115	2,320	2,600	5,030	3,485	18,190
CASH POSITION	71,455	69,135	61,675	59,670	60,022	60,752	60,062	62,177	64,497	61,097	68,037	71,512	

NOTES:

GM %	30% x sales	
Royalty	5% multiply X sales	
Ad Fund	2% multiply X sales	
Total expenses		
Total cash plus GM dollars		
GN dollars minus total expenses	#NAME?	

Figure 4.1 Sample Pro Forma Income Statement and Cash Flow.

Final Check

Once these evaluations have been completed, the final step is contending with any unanticipated barriers that would jeopardize the implementation of the franchise program. There can always be sudden changes in the business world that may disrupt the best-laid plans of companies seeking to implement new business strategies such as franchising. When this occurs, a company must seriously consider pausing its franchise program. Failing to respond can have a negative impact on the launch and implementation of a new franchise program and company operations.

Examples of factors that could cause a company to pause its franchise program include the following:

External Factors
- New franchise regulations at the federal or state level may require certain qualifications before a franchisor can offer new franchises for sale. For example, the state in which the company operates may require franchisors to register their documents, such as New York or California.
- A catastrophic event such as a pandemic. At the end of 2020 continuing into 2021, the unanticipated arrival of the COVID-19 pandemic had a devastating impact on world economies and countless businesses.
- A severe economic downturn, such as a recession, can limit the desire of individuals to risk investing in a franchise. Although history has revealed that certain recessions have maintained franchise activity, this is not a large enough sample to render a statistically accurate prediction.

Internal Factors
- A financial, management or operational disruption within the company could directly impact the success of the franchise project.
- A significant competitive event in a strategic market or region could disrupt new franchise recruitment and development activities.
- If the company doesn't have a thorough trademark search done and it turns out another company has prior rights to the same trademark in other states, the company might need a new trademark or avoid franchising in conflicting states.

A careful examination of these aspects in the evaluation process will uncover potential problems the company may encounter if it decides to construct and launch a new franchise program. If a problem is found after the evaluation is completed, potential franchisors should address these problems before proceeding. One way to avoid overlooking potential obstacles to building and launching a successful franchise program is to seek objective input from qualified individuals including franchise consultants, company CFO, Board of Directors, or financial advisors, by providing the chance to review and critique the franchise project. If the five aspects of franchise evaluation are favorable and indicate the franchise venture should proceed, potential franchisors may take the next step, presented in Chapter 5.

Summary

Before committing to a franchise program, potential franchisors should conduct an in-depth evaluation of the qualifications the company has for a franchise operation. This evaluation process could start with a thought experiment comparing franchising with other growth strategies. Franchisers should then carefully examine the five key aspects of franchise evaluation that require franchisors to conduct internal feasibility analysis and investigate whether there are sufficient internal capabilities and resources to plan and implement franchising strategies. They should also examine whether the core business can be easily franchisable.

In addition, potential franchisors need to scrutinize industries to identify existing competitors and best practices. Potential franchisors should estimate the return on investment for helpful information to gauge the interest of potential franchisees. They should follow with a final examination of unanticipated barriers that could prevent the launch and implementation of a new franchise system. Analysis and conclusions regarding whether a company should franchise represents a decision process that should be separated from the determination of type, method, and timing of a new franchise program. If the evaluations of these aspects are positive, potential franchisors could proceed to building and launching the new franchise program.

Companies that qualify for establishing and launching a franchise program should be well managed, profitable operations with an attractive product or service, preferably multiple locations, suitable investment capital, and competent management. Their product or service should appeal to customers and there must be reliable financial projections that present a realistic projection of a profitable franchise operation. In the next chapter, we present the steps and requirements for building a new franchise program.

Notes

1 Delmar, F., & Shane, S. (2003). Does business planning facilitate the development of new ventures? *Strategic Management Journal*, 24(12), 1165–1185.

2 Brinckmann, J., Grichnik, D., & Kapsa, D. (2010). Should entrepreneurs plan or just storm the castle? A meta-analysis on contextual factors impacting the business planning–performance relationship in small firms. *Journal of Business Venturing, 25*(1), 24–40.

3 Brinckmann, J., Grichnik, D., & Kapsa, D. (2010). Should entrepreneurs plan or just storm the castle? A meta-analysis on contextual factors impacting the business planning – performance relationship in small firms. *Journal of Business Venturing, 25*(1), 24–40.

4 Spencer, E. (2006). Franchising – A way to supersize a business. *The National Legal Eagle, 12*(1), Article 2. Available at: http://epublications.bond.edu.au/nle/vol12/iss1/2

5 Hussain, D., Sreckovic, M., & Windsperger, J. (2018). An organizational capability perspective on multi-unit franchising. *Small Business Economics, 50*(4), 717–727. Gillis, W. E., Combs, J. G., & Ketchen Jr., D. J. (2014). Using resource-based theory to help explain plural form franchising. *Entrepreneurship Theory and Practice, 38*(3), 449–472.

6 Keller, K. L. (2003). Brand synthesis: The multidimensionality of brand knowledge. *Journal of Consumer Research, 29*(4), 595–600. Ailawadi, K. L., Lehmann, D. R., & Neslin, S. A. (2003). Revenue premium as an outcome measure of brand equity. *Journal of Marketing, 67*(4), 1–17. Litz, R. A., & Stewart, A. C. (1998). Franchising for sustainable advantage? Comparing the performance of independent retailers and trade-name franchisees. *Journal of Business Venturing, 13*(2), 131–150.

7 Gillis, W. E., Combs, J. G., & Ketchen Jr., D. J. (2014). Using resource-based theory to help explain plural form franchising. *Entrepreneurship Theory and Practice, 38*(3), 449–472. Kaufmann, P. J., & Dant, R. P. (1996). Multi-unit franchising: Growth and management issues. *Journal of Business Venturing, 11*(5), 343–358. Shane, S. (1998). Explaining the distribution of franchised and company-owned outlets in franchise systems. *Journal of Management, 24*(6), 717–739.

8 Butt, M. N., Antia, K. D., Murtha, B. R., & Kashyap, V. (2018). Clustering, knowledge sharing, and intrabrand competition: A multiyear analysis of an evolving franchise system. *Journal of Marketing, 82*(1), 74–92.

9 Kaufmann, P. J., & Eroglu, S. (1999). Standardization and adaptation in business format franchising. *Journal of Business Venturing, 14*(1), 69–85. Sorenson, O., & Sørensen, J. B. (2001). Finding the right mix: Franchising, organizational learning, and chain performance. *Strategic Management Journal, 22*(6–7), 713–724.

Chapter 5

Preparing for New Franchise Launch

In Chapter 4, we presented the process that potential franchisors should follow to determine if they have the qualifications and resources to design and execute a franchise business model. This is the initial step in the implementation of a franchising strategy; the process involves five major evaluation aspects that can enable potential franchisors to determine the feasibility of a franchising strategy. If the results confirm that the company and its business operation have met the qualifications necessary to franchise, the next step is to design and build the new franchise.

This chapter discusses the preliminary activities that can help potential franchisors prepare for the launch of a franchise business. These activities are essential, given the legal requirements that franchisors must address in order to prevent a potential fiasco. Such activities can also help explain important franchising business and legal documents, and guide the franchise business development.

Launching a franchise program can be a daunting task, because the franchising process requires a comprehensive understanding of rules and regulations, and involves a set of complex activities ranging from the standardization of business operations to franchisee recruitment, training, and management. Many franchisors may not possess the knowledge and skill sets required, and must seek help from relevant stakeholders, so it is important for them to recognize groups of advisors who can bring value-added knowledge and skills to the franchise development process.

Next, we discuss securing trademarks, registering website domain names, and incorporating the new franchise system. We then highlight four vital documents: the Franchise Operations Manual, Franchise Disclosure Document, Franchise Agreement, and Franchise Business Model. These are areas that potential franchisors should be familiar with. They are often legally required and can also guide franchisors in constructing their business model. We conclude with a discussion by franchising professionals who may assist potential franchisors with the design and construction of their franchise programs.

DOI: 10.4324/9781003034285-5

Securing Trademarks and Website Domain Names

The name of the company and its website domain are important, as these are often the first pieces of information that external stakeholders such as customers, investors, and franchisees encounter; they have been proven to significantly influence how stakeholders evaluate and view a company.[1] Studies have found that companies that have easily pronounceable names are perceived to be more familiar and less risky, offer better returns, and achieve higher value in the stock market.[2] Names that are less frequently used in a particular language may result in positive evaluations, especially in early-stage ventures.[3] The designs of logos and trademarks have also been shown to influence evaluations.[4] Taken together, such studies suggest that potential franchisors should carefully consider names of a company and website domain, and how the logo and trademark should be designed.

As indicated in Chapter 4, potential franchisors should make sure names and trademarks have not been used nor previously registered by other companies. Otherwise, they may have to rename their company or redesign logos and trademarks. Properly registering names and trademarks will ensure that they are conflict-free and fully protected. A domain name that echoes the trademark should also be secured. A potential franchisor should acquire a domain name with the suffix .com, .org, .us, and .biz to avoid conflicts and competitive encroachment on domain names that may be confused with the franchise name. The cost to acquire additional domain names is minor compared to the potential damage from another company, competitor, or franchisor using the same name with a different suffix. If there are plans to go international, potential franchisors may wish to consult with a trademark attorney about the registration of trademarks and domains in specific countries.

Incorporating the Franchise Corporation

Once the trademark and domain names have been properly acquired and registered, the next step is to incorporate a new and independent company to operate the franchise system and create, advise, and manage franchise units. Although the original company may be incorporated, it is considered best practice for potential franchisors to operate under a new corporation. First, doing so will avoid potential conflicts or financial entanglements with the existing corporation because they will be separate entities, and any assets, liabilities, and equity will be held by individual entities. This will make it difficult for claims to be made against the company for acts under the franchisor corporation, and may insulate the original company from future claims or litigation that pertain to the franchisor. Finally, because audited financial statements for the franchise corporation are required to be included in legal documents, having a newly capitalized corporation with minimal financial history will reduce the cost of audited financial statements, which may be substantial if the company has a number of financial transactions.

Choosing between Two Franchise Development Models

It is important to choose a franchise development model. It will affect what types of franchise candidates should be targeted, and how and where to recruit them. The most prevalent franchise development model is the single-unit franchisee, where an individual purchases the rights to open a franchise unit. The structure consists of a franchisee owner-operator who is responsible for the day-to-day operations of the franchise. Examples include homecare, landscaping, and children's services, which require only a modest investment and do not generate enough income to fund a manager along with an owner-operator. The single-unit franchise development model takes longer to grow locations, because each transaction results in one franchise. A franchise system comprised of single-unit franchises requires additional support personnel because they will be dealing with numerous individual franchisees.

An alternative development model is the multi-unit franchisee, where a franchisee or group of franchisees acquire the rights to own and operate several locations. The multi-unit franchisee is the preferred strategy in sit-down and quick-service restaurant sectors, which require a substantial investment and highly qualified franchise candidates. A multi-unit franchisee will agree to open multiple locations in a specific territory. The advantages of a multi-unit strategy include faster system growth, quicker brand recognition, and the ability to purchase products and services at a reduced cost due to increased buying power. Most multi-unit franchisees utilize franchise managers, with the franchisee overseeing the overall operation. An advantage of the multi-unit model is that support staff deals with fewer franchisees who control multiple locations.

Certain franchise models are better suited to specific types of franchises, depending upon the operation, amount of investment, and potential earnings. Beginning with the unit franchise, a franchisor can better support a franchisee because they are operating at a single location. Also, it may be difficult for a startup franchisor to attract candidates willing to invest substantial capital into an unproven franchise. Some franchisors offer unit franchise and multi-unit models in their Franchise Disclosure Document in the event an investor sees a good opportunity investing in multiple units of the new franchise and committing substantial capital. While startup franchisors initially tend to launch a franchise using the unit franchise model, some systems may offer a multi-unit opportunity to prospective franchisees who have successfully managed single units after 2 years or have sufficient resources to open a minimum of ten units. Ultimately, the franchisor must be sure that the opportunity is sufficiently appealing that potential franchisees will want to own several units.

Understanding Essential Franchise Documents

Building a franchise system requires documents that will form the basis of the contractual relationship between franchisors and franchisees. It enables franchisors to record their business activities and effectively communicate with potential franchisees. Some documents are legally required. To prepare for a new franchise business, it is important to understand the basic outline and key components as these help potential franchisors prepare for building a franchise system. Next, we discuss four major franchise documents: the Franchise Operations Manual, Disclosure Document, Franchise Agreement, and Franchise Business Plan.

The Franchise Operations Manual

The Franchise Operations Manual, often referred to as the Manual, contains the systems, procedures, and guidelines that assist and direct franchisees in their operation. It also presents several checklists for franchisees to examine key aspects of site selection, employee recruitment, competitive analysis, and marketing evaluation.

The Manual serves three purposes. It acts as a training tool and provides content for the initial training program. It helps franchisees to understand the proper operation of their franchise unit by laying out the specific materials and exact procedures needed to create products and/or services. Its second purpose is to ensure franchise compliance and maintain consistent product/service quality across business units. Operations Manuals depict specific standards and procedures of business operations; the Manual is referenced in several legally binding franchise documents, and thus prevail as the determining factor in case of operational disputes between a franchisor and its franchisees. Finally, creation of a Franchise Operations Manual offers potential franchisors the opportunity to organize, standardize, and document the existing company or pilot operation.

It is common for a smaller company to lack written procedures and training programs, so once the franchise has been confirmed as a feasible growth strategy, potential franchisors should systematically compile this information for the development of an Operations Manual. The Manual must be organized so that the franchisee has a template for how the business will be operated. If necessary, franchisors may consult with companies that specialize in producing Manuals. A Manual may be or can be 75–150 pages long and cost $10,000 to $25,000 or more to compile.

The typical Operations Manual often consists of 10–12 sections. According to Collin Gaffney, President of FranStart which specializes in producing franchise manuals, the Operations Manual may consist of several sections or separate topical manuals that include a pre-opening or startup manual, as well as marketing and human resource manuals. A sample of the typical sections is shown in the following example of an Operations Manual from a retail franchise that serves snacks and beverages. The chapters are an example of those found in many Operations Manuals for different types of franchise systems.

Sample Operations Manual

TABLE OF CONTENTS

Welcome from the President. This occurs at the beginning of the Operations Manual where the President of the Franchiser presents a letter welcoming the new franchisee and providing a description of the mission statement and corporate culture to personalize the franchise–franchisor relationship. The welcome letter adds a personal touch to the franchisor-franchisee relationship and may be short or long, depending upon the message to be conveyed.

Chapter 1. Introduction: This chapter provides a brief preview of what to expect from the manual and highlights its confidential nature. Franchisees are informed that they must update the manual when notified. The introduction often recaps important obligations under the franchise agreement including a non-disclosure document.

Chapter 2. Human Resources: This chapter presents employee job descriptions, recruiting suggestions, and employment practices and policies that franchisees must adhere to. This section contains recommended approaches for managing human resources and understanding labor regulations. Such knowledge and practices when implemented will prevent the brand from suffering negative publicity due to poor human resource management.

Chapter 3. Daily Operating Procedures: This chapter includes hours of operation, preparation for daily opening, closing, reconciling sales receipts, and securing the premises. These operating procedures enable franchise units to standardize operations and create an identical customer experience.

Chapter 4. Product Handling and Sanitation: This chapter describes how products should be received, stored, and maintained in compliance with expiration codes. It presents the requirements for complying with product storage, sanitation, and freshness coding. These procedures insure that product quality remain consistent across franchise units and prevents potential hazards resulting from faulty product usage or consumption.

Chapter 5. Customer Service: This chapter illustrates how to respond and resolve customer complaints and problems related to product quality, sales refunds, and other customer service issues. Franchise systems receive customer complaints from time to time, but most issues can be anticipated. It is imperative to devise procedures for how to handle these issues such as making sure that franchisees have the proper tools and guidelines to resolve complaints, improve customer satisfaction, and attract returning customers.

Chapter 6. Gross Profit and Inventory: This chapter explains procedures for product pricing, calculating gross profit, and maintaining proper inventory levels. In certain industries, franchisees are required to establish retail prices based on their competitors and the gross margin. This can help franchisees, especially those who lack a financial background or have difficulty maximizing their gross margins, to derive a good pricing strategy by understanding whether and by how much they may reduce prices and what impact this will have on the gross margin for that product.

Chapter 7. Cash Handling: This chapter sets forth point of sale terminals, commonly referred to as cash registers, so that franchisors may uniformly record all sales transactions and reports. Many point of sales terminals used by franchisees, especially in the retail sector, allow the franchisor to download data directly from the terminals. This chapter often cites the obligation of the franchisee to register all customer sales or face violation of their franchise agreement.

Chapter 8. Marketing & Advertising: This chapter describes the marketing programs recommended by the franchisor, the proper use of franchise trademarks, and the approval process of franchise-created advertising. It may include various forms of advertising, such as use of social media. This is an important chapter, as use of unauthorized advertising vehicles or statements may damage or dilute the image and reputation of the entire brand. Most franchisors strictly control and restrict the use of social media and the brand by franchisees.

Chapter 9. Financial Reporting: This chapter describes monthly, quarterly, and/or annual financial reports that franchisees are required to provide. It states the obligation to submit tax returns, financial reports and supporting documents to the franchisor, information that may enable the franchisor to identify and measure how well franchisees are performing. Once a franchisor recognizes that certain franchisees are not profitable, they can provide appropriate staff to turn around struggling franchises.

Chapter 10. Forms: This chapter presents examples of required forms that need to be used by franchisees and highlights those that must be submitted to the franchisor. The purpose of the chapter is to ensure that all franchisees are consistently using the same forms such as job applications, supplier requests, and customer incident reports.

The Operations Manual is usually created in tandem with the Franchise Disclosure Document (FDD) because certain provisions are based on and reference the FDD. Most Franchise Operations Manuals are provided digitally, although some franchisors may provide hard copies upon request. Provisions and requirements in the Operations Manual must be amended from time to time, except for certain contractual items such as the royalty fees, termination provisions, etc. These changes or updates need to be shared with franchisees who are then responsible to make any changes or updates.

The Franchise Disclosure Document

The Franchise Disclosure Document (FDD) is one of the most important franchise documents and must be carefully drafted. It is part of presale due diligence and is required to be given to a franchise candidate by the Federal Trade Commission. Based in part on U.S. securities laws, the FDD must provide every prospective franchisee in every state information about the franchisor, the franchise system, and agreements with which a franchisee must comply. The FDD should enable a franchise prospect to make an informed investment decision. A franchise candidate must be provided with an FDD 14 calendar days prior to signing a franchise agreement or paying money for a franchise. A franchisor is obligated to have the prospective franchisee sign, date, and return the acknowledgment of receipt to the franchisor to confirm that these were properly disclosed. The required disclosure of the FDD is the same whether a franchisor is large or small, established or new. The format of required disclosure has been revised several times by the Federal Trade Commission and certain states in order to provide meaningful disclosure to prospective franchisees and require that franchisors provide specific items such as the franchise territory, litigation, and financial performance representations in their disclosure document. The FDD refers to specific provisions in the franchise agreement. Typically, a prospective franchisee and his/her attorney will review the FDD before reading the franchise agreement, because it contains the most important parts of the franchise agreement. It can be considered a synopsis of the franchise agreement.

There are 22 categories in the FDD, known as items. These disclose relevant information in what is referred to as simple English, a change enacted in 1979 to prevent inflicting overly legal language on individuals. Some items are informational such as Litigation, Bankruptcy, Trademarks, and Public Figures, which require little or no decision-making on the part of the potential franchisors and their franchise attorneys. Other items deal with operational and financial areas specific to the franchise which require potential franchisors to carefully analyze and consult with an attorney. These include other fees, Franchisee's Obligations, and Territory. There are several exhibits in the FDD. One of the most important is the Franchise Agreement, which contains the covenants and franchisee and franchisor obligations that form the franchise relationship and is the binding contract that both parties will sign. The provisions in the franchise agreement include franchise fees, term of the franchise agreement, territory, insurance requirements, ongoing operations, and the basis for default and termination of the agreement. Because the franchise relationship may potentially involve conflicts and disagreements between parties, it is important there are vehicles to resolve disputes in the franchise agreement, such as mediation and arbitration, which can avoid costly litigation.[5] Other exhibits include the table of contents for the operations manual, non-compete and non-disclosure agreements, and franchisor financial statements.

Based on our experience, and discussion with prominent franchise attorneys, there are eight FDD items that may require further explanation.

Item 5: Franchising Model

The franchising business model is used to develop the franchise system. The two most popular models are the unit franchise and multi-franchise. In the unit model, the franchisee acquires the rights to one location within the territory, which may be a separate or home-based location. According to several industry sources, including the International Franchise Association, unit franchises represent approximately 70% of all franchises. The unit franchise model is important because it conforms to most franchise concepts that require an onsite owner-operator, because there are not enough profits to justify a passive owner, that is, a person who doesn't work in the franchise.

A multi-unit franchise grants the right and obligation to own and operate several franchise locations in multiple territories under separate franchise agreements according to a schedule; this is the model preferred by food franchisors. This is an important franchise model for franchisees who desire to own multiple franchise units and can justify paying the salary of a manager. Several years ago, Mcdonald's transitioned to a multi-unit franchise model.

Item 5: Initial Franchise Fee

This item highlights the fees a franchisee must pay before a franchised business opens for business. It includes franchise rights, use of the brand, training, operations manual, and grand opening support. The average franchise fees range from $25,000 to 50,000. When determining the initial franchise fee, startups should charge fees comparable to those charged by competitors. This is an important item in the FDD because prospective franchisees compare the amount of the Initial Franchise Fee to other franchises. When an individual questions the amount of the initial fee, they want to know what they are receiving in return.

Item 6: Royalties and Other Fees

One of the more important Items describes continuing fees that the franchisee is obligated to pay as stipulated in the franchise agreement. These fees can be based on a percent of revenues, a fixed dollar amount, or a combination of both.

A startup franchisor without an established reputation may face problems attracting franchisees because potential franchisees do not know if the value of the system is going to be high enough to justify the royalty rate they have to pay the franchisor. Systems with lower royalty rates will find it easier to attract franchisees than those with higher royalty rates. The lower the royalty rate, the greater the chance that the system value will be high enough to justify a royalty rate.[6]

Item 7: Estimated Initial Investment

The franchisor must disclose minimum and maximum investments of all fees, costs, and expenses that a franchisee will incur prior to operating the franchised business. The Federal Trade Commission requires that a franchisor know and specify the range of franchisee investments. This item enables franchisees to understand the cost structure of launching and managing a franchise unit so they can get a realistic preview of the financial management of their franchise units. Franchisers should provide a reasonable basis for each category when citing estimated costs, and state in general terms the basis they relied upon to calculate estimated additional funds, including local market variations in price and annually updated figures, to ensure they are providing accurate numbers.[7]

Item 9: Franchisee's Obligations

Item 9 discloses principal obligations for operating a franchise. This item is essential, as the highlighted obligations, which are also presented in the franchise agreement, are legally binding. Franchisees will be placed in default of their agreement, or their unit may be terminated from the franchise if these obligations are not fulfilled and followed closely. Such information is required by the Federal Trade Commission and registration states.

Franchisee's obligations are presented in a three-column table which references the franchise agreement or other relevant agreements as well as the item in the FDD where more information about a particular obligation can be found. Examples include site location, fees, restrictions on products or services, advertising, and location appearance. Unlike other items in the FDD, Item 9 does not contain specific details regarding franchisee obligations but rather cites sections in the franchise agreement where a description is contained.

Item 11: Franchiser Obligations

One of the lengthier and more important disclosure items is the franchisor obligations, including the services it provides to franchisees. Like Item 9, franchisor obligations, once listed in the franchise agreement, are legally binding. With this knowledge, prospective franchisees not only know the specific services and assistance they will receive from a franchisor, they can compare them with other franchise systems. Important franchisor obligations include pre-opening and site selection assistance, training programs, advertising programs, the minimum number of visits a franchisor will make to the franchisee location, and provided counseling.

Item 12: Territory

This item describes the territory where franchisee customers, revenues, and future growth will originate. A franchisee territory may be exclusive, protected, or open. If the territory is too small, generating revenue can be difficult, and franchisees must compete for customers within a territory. This is an important consideration for franchise candidates. In some programs, a franchisee can be on the border of another territory and must vie for the customers in that territory.

Although often used interchangeably, "exclusive" and "protected" territories have different meanings within a franchise context. If a franchise territory is exclusive, the business should be the only source of goods or services in the territory. If a franchisee territory is protected, the franchise agreement may authorize certain forms of competition such as franchisor sales through alternative channels of distribution (i.e., the internet and supermarkets).[8]

Item 19: Financial Performance Representation

Under Federal Trade Commission rules, information about the financial performance of a franchise such as average franchisee revenues or profits can only be disclosed in Item 19 to be given to a prospective franchisee. For startup franchisors without previous franchisee financial information, franchisors should disclose company-level financial performance information. This is very important, as franchisees typically want to know how much they may expect to earn if they invest in a particular franchise. Franchisers need to identify specific type of financial information relevant to their business and industry. For example, a hotel franchise system may use occupancy rates as a key financial indicator, while restaurant systems include gross sales figures and key percentages reflecting food or labor costs, and car wash businesses offer daily car counts and average ticket numbers.[9]

The Franchise Agreement

An essential franchise document is the Franchise Agreement, a legally binding document executed by franchisor and franchisee which sets forth what a franchisee is obligated to do in the operation of their franchise and what a franchisor is obligated to do to support franchisees. Certain obligations and requirements may be amended or clarified in the Franchise Operations Manual, excluding material provisions of the franchise agreement such as royalty payments, fees, franchise term and renewal, and default and termination provisions.

Although franchise agreements follow a certain format, there is no standard form of franchise agreement because the terms, conditions, and methods of operations of various franchises may vary, depending on the type of franchise. A franchise attorney will insert provisions and requirements into the franchise agreement that conform to the specific franchise concept. While there may be some overlap between the Franchise Agreement and the FDD, they are two distinct documents. Unlike the FDD, which provides an overview and description of key components of the franchise program, the franchise agreement goes into detail to elucidate all aspects of the franchisee/franchisor relationship. This includes information regarding operational standards, proprietary statements, and franchisee responsibilities such as site maintenance, remodeling requirements, and franchisee financial obligations.

Examples of important Franchise Agreement Provisions that are common to all franchise agreements include the following:

a   Grant of the Franchise describes the franchise and products or services it provides, the products a franchisee is allowed to sell and the product/service characteristics that must be maintained in order to achieve system-wide standards.
b   The Franchise Territory describes the area a franchise can operate within, where franchisees can open a location and sell their products or services. It can prevent potential conflicts among franchisees. For example, a franchisee that does medical staffing for hospitals could enter another franchisee's territory and solicit business. With

    territorial protections, franchisors can prevent this from happening and protect the franchise system and brand.

c   The Franchise Term states the length of an initial franchise and renewal terms. Franchise terms can range from 5 years to as long as 20 years, in the case of hotel and certain fast-food franchises. The most common franchise term is 10 years with a 5-year renewal term.

d   Royalties and fees specify the amount of money the franchisee is obligated to pay along with frequency and payment method. It contractually binds a franchisee to pay royalty and other fees on a continuing basis. The basis of a franchisee-franchisor relationship is royalties a franchisee must pay for the right to operate under the franchise brand, operating system, and territory. Examples may state that a franchisee agrees to pay a 5% royalty on all gross sales each month, based on the previous month's sales.

e   Franchisee Insurance Requirements describe the insurance coverage, amount of coverage, and required credentials of the insurance carrier, such as AAA rated. It is important that each franchisee has insurance to protect its franchise from losses due to events such as a fire or hurricane. One example of franchisee insurance coverage is Business Interruption Coverage, which protects a franchisee from business losses due to a fire or natural disaster.

f   Franchise Opening describes how many days before a franchise opens for business. This can depend on the complexity of the franchise. A hotel franchisee may have 1 year to open due to extensive construction requirements, while a fast-food franchise may be required to open within 6 months. If a franchisee can open any time it wants, the franchise system would lack sufficient order. Franchisees are required to open their franchise within a specific period of time; otherwise, the franchisor could terminate the franchise and grant the franchise rights to someone else.

g   Franchisee Defaults details the specific items under which a franchise can be placed in default of their franchise agreement, how many days are required to cure the default; if not cured, the franchise may be terminated. This is a clause required by Federal Trade Commission. Franchisees must recognize in a legal form that certain actions on their part can jeopardize their franchisee rights, for example, if a franchisee fails to open their business within a certain number of days. The most common default provision occurs when the franchisee lacks sufficient funds to pay their royalty fees.

While certain details in the FDD may change as the franchise system grows, the franchise agreement will change very little in order to allow all franchisees to operate under the same obligations and be treated fairly. While the franchise agreement should balance the interests of franchisor and franchisee, the agreement must provide certain rights to the franchisor so it can uphold and enforce the overall standards of the franchise system; otherwise, a franchisee could sell unauthorized products or services, or operate in an unlicensed location. These actions could hurt the franchise brand and other franchisees, and are another reason why franchisees deserve a strong franchise agreement.

The Franchise Business Plan

As franchise documents are being constructed, work should commence on the franchise business plan. When a potential franchisor is involved in building the franchise program, questions may arise regarding the development and growth of the franchise system. These subjects should be included in the Franchise Business Plan.

The franchise business plan represents an important strategic document that describes and summarizes how a new franchisor will meet its operational and financial goals. When planning a new franchise program, the business plan will outline key steps necessary to launch and build a successful franchise network. The business plan can be used to raise capital and prompt franchise management to answer questions pertaining to the franchise venture. A business plan can help manage the franchise operation and identify important timelines and goals. Without a business plan, a potential franchisor would lack a detailed plan to navigate the launch and development of a successful franchise.

The following components should be included in a franchise business plan:

a   The Executive Summary: This should be short and concise – one page is ideal. It is perhaps the most important section, as most readers often do not read the entire plan. It should include a brief overview of the business strategy and describe the franchise product or service, market and major competitors, why the product or service has promise, and what distinguishes them from other franchises.

b   Franchise Concept: This section describes the core business idea of the franchise system and what makes it appealing. It should explain what sets the business apart from the competition. A reader should be able to understand the products or services a franchise will offer its customers and how these may differ from those of competitors.

c   Franchise Leadership: This section highlights individual profiles of the management team and specifies key responsibilities. It may describe the characteristics of the management team that contribute to the success of the franchise launch and development. This information signals the underlying quality of a franchise business and enables potential investors or lenders to know who will be leading the organization and their experience and accomplishments.

d The Market: This section describes the potential market size and specifies the local or national scope and strategies that a franchise system will focus on in company-operated locations. Most importantly, it highlights the trends in a particular market and whether the market is growing, stable, or shrinking.

e Competition: This section contains an in-depth analysis of potential competitors, including both franchise systems and non-franchise businesses. It highlights the strengths and weaknesses of competitors and elaborates on how potential franchisees may deal with them effectively by highlighting counter strategies and approaches to allay major concerns that may hinder success.

f Product features and benefits: This section describes the key features of the franchise, products, or services. It is important to be clear not only about distinguishing features of a product or service but to delineate customer benefits. Ultimately franchisees need to know what makes their product or service better than competitive offerings so they can market these to potential consumers.

g Brand strategy: This describes the marketing plan for the franchise, highlighting how the franchise will be marketed, to whom, and where. This is an important element because it describes the specific methods used to develop brand recognition.

h Franchise Development: This is a critical and unique component of the franchise business plan that presents a strategy for growing the franchise system. It should provide an overview of the marketing strategy for developing a franchise network, targeted markets and advertising, and promotional programs used to recruit qualified candidates.

i Financial Projections: This section should include franchisor and franchisee pro forma financials which include projected revenue/income streams: This is an important component of any business plan because it represents projected cash flow and income statements, i.e., how much a franchise stands to earn.

Considering Franchise Advisors

The process of building a franchise system is complex and may require assistance from professionals who have experience in the franchise industry. With the requisite skills, qualifications, and experience, these individuals can help potential franchisors design and build a franchise program effectively and efficiently, draft franchise documents, and deal with franchisor-franchisee disputes and other challenges and problems that startup franchisors may face. Next, we discuss two groups of advisors from whom potential franchisors often seek help.

The Franchise Attorney

The franchise attorney is one of the most important members of the franchise team. Because the franchise industry is regulated by the Federal Trade Commission and several states, it is important to consult with an attorney familiar with franchisor compliance, regulatory requirements, and the franchise business model. Many qualified franchise attorneys can be found on the internet or listed on the websites of franchise-related entities, such as the International Franchise Association. You may also consult with your own attorney, accounting firms, and franchise consultants to identify a qualified franchise attorney. It is important to conduct a thorough evaluation and speak with previous clients to determine if an attorney is the right fit for your franchise service. Questions may include legal fees, responsiveness to requests for information, feedback regarding the quality of the franchise documents, and duration for completing franchise forms.

After an attorney has been chosen to review franchise documents, they should meet with the potential franchise principals for an in-depth discussion of the business being franchised and its objectives, size, and timing related to the launch of the franchise network. An attorney will often provide an overview of the franchise process, ask questions regarding the franchise operation, and recommend how a franchise should be structured. Some franchise attorneys present the advantages and disadvantages of launching and implementing a franchise program to confirm that their clients understand and are committed to a franchising strategy. At the end of an initial meeting, the attorney will present their fee structure and the services they provide. Most franchise law firms have a fixed fee for their services, including the production of franchise documents and required ancillary services. These can range from $15,000–30,000. Potential franchisors should avoid being "penny wise and pound foolish" and not choose a law firm primarily based on cost. Such a cost-saving strategy could be detrimental in the long run, because poorly constructed documents can create numerous problems that will be expensive to fix, once the new franchise program is launched and franchisees brought onboard.

Once an engagement letter is signed with the attorney, the law firm will send the potential franchisor a detailed questionnaire for franchisors to complete and return. Such a questionnaire asks for preliminary information about the new franchise including its operation, projected franchisee investment, initial franchise fee, royalties, and other information necessary to prepare the documents. The franchise attorney may suggest that the potential franchisor obtain the services of a consultant regarding important business decisions that require industry knowledge.

The Franchise Consultant

Most franchise consultants have experience as a franchise executive or former owner of a franchise company, so they understand the process of launching and implementing a franchising strategy. Their services can be quite helpful, particularly when potential franchisors do not have substantial experience with the system. Not engaging a qualified franchise consultant or choosing the wrong one can cost a potential franchisor time and money, and may negatively affect the quality of the entire franchise program, leaving franchisors with less capital to launch and develop the new program. Due diligence is needed when choosing a franchise consultant.

As with a capable franchise attorney, it is important to evaluate the competence and qualifications of a consultant. The best way to evaluate the qualifications of a consultant is to contact past clients and contact and evaluate the quality and cost of their services. When seeking feedback on a franchise consultant, potential franchisors should ask about the cost of the consultant, their business style, franchise knowledge, and if they had to do it again, if they would use that consultant again.

A franchise consultant offers advice on the non-legal components of franchising, such as how to determine the initial franchise fee, royalties, and structure the franchise territory. He or she should have experience recruiting franchise candidates, marketing and operating procedures, and franchise relations. In addition, a franchise consultant should know how to acquire competitive franchise information to assist the potential franchisor in designing competing strategies. Some franchise use consultants as a staff member who can provide marketing services and construct training manuals.

Summary

This chapter describes the process of preparing a new franchise launch. We have discussed the importance of securing trademarks, registering website domain names, and incorporating the new franchise system. We described the outline and key aspects of four important franchise documents, including the Franchise Operations Manual, Franchise Disclosure Document, Franchise Agreement, and Franchise Business Model. We concluded by highlighting important considerations for recruiting franchise professionals who will assist in building the new franchise, including the franchise attorney, franchise consultant, and accountant.

Taken together, these activities will prepare potential franchisors in launching their new franchise system by setting up legal protections that will help to avoid preventable fiascos, understanding the franchise business, providing legal documents to guide franchise business development, and recognizing groups of potential franchise advisors who can provide insights and tools that improve the efficiency and effectiveness of the franchise development process.

Notes

1 Alter, A. L., & Oppenheimer, D. M. (2006). Predicting short-term stock fluctuations by using processing fluency. *Proceedings of the National Academy of Sciences, 103*(24), 9369–9372.
2 Green, T. C., & James, R. (2013). Company name fluency, investor recognition, and firm value. *Journal of Financial Economics, 109*(3), 813–834.
3 Chan, C. S. R., Park, H. D., & Patel, P. (2018). The effect of company name fluency on venture investment decisions and IPO underpricing. *Venture Capital, 20*(1), 1–26.
4 Mahmood, A., Luffarelli, J., & Mukesh, M. (2019). What's in a logo? The impact of complex visual cues in equity crowdfunding. *Journal of Business Venturing, 34*(1), 41–62.
5 Leblebici, H., & Shalley, C. E. (1996). The organization of relational contracts: The allocation of rights in franchising. *Journal of Business Venturing, 11*(5), 403–418.
6 Calderon-Monge, E., Pastor-Sanz, I., & Huerta-Zavala, P. (2017). *Economic sustainability in franchising: A model to predict franchisor success or failure.* Department of Economics and Business Administration, University of Burgos, Burgos, Spain; pp. 1–5.
7 Lusthaus, J. *How Do You Determine the Initial Investment for the Item.* https://lusthausfranchiselaw.com/blog/how-do-you-determine-the-initial-investment-for-the-fdd/
8 Teixeira, E. (2018). Understanding key aspects of the franchise territory. *Forbes.* https://www.forbes.com/sites/edteixeira/2018/05/31/understand-key-aspects-of-the-franchise-territory/
9 Caffey, A. The importance of item 19 in the franchise disclosure document. *All Business.* https://www.allbusiness.com/the-importance-of-item-19-in-the-franchise-disclosure-document-13425632-1.html

Chapter 6

Developing Franchisor Organizational Capabilities

In Chapter 5, we presented the process for preparing the launch of a franchise program and the resources necessary to accomplish that objective. During the period between the completion of the franchise documents and the launch of the franchise development program, the franchisor must establish the structure and hire the staff that can recruit, develop, and support new franchisees combined with the required financial and operational controls. To accomplish these objectives, the franchisor must create and strengthen their organizational capabilities.

In this chapter, we delineate the blueprint for establishing the organizational structure and capabilities for the franchisor to effectively operate and manage its franchise system. This is an important step for developing a franchise program because potential franchisors need to build up the internal capability to train, support, and assist franchisees. Otherwise, franchisees and the franchise program could fail easily as poorly qualified staff would not be able to fulfill the franchisors' contractual obligations, resulting in ineffective management of the franchisor–franchisee relationships.

Next, we present three possible configurations of franchisor organizational structures as these could differ drastically depending upon the size and stage of the franchise systems. We then delineate and discuss key top management team members (the "TMT") who would essentially establish, provide, and administer franchise operational systems. Finally, because most startup franchisors emerge from small companies there may be a need to engage outside resources to provide specific services to the franchisor until the franchise system reaches a certain size. We conclude by illustrating several potential service areas, such as marketing and Information Technology supports, that franchisors may wish to outsource at the initial startup process.

DOI: 10.4324/9781003034285-6

Three Examples of Franchisor Organizational Structure

The franchisor organizational structure highlights the key positions, functional areas, and reporting relationships in the franchisor organization. This is important because such structure not only provides a blueprint on the reporting relationships among employees, but also illustrates how organizational resources are being assembled and orchestrated to achieve organizational performance.[1]

Further, franchisor organizational structures can differ depending upon the size of the franchise system and the number of supporting resources to be offered to its franchisees. It is important for the franchisor to incorporate the important members of its TMT and support staff in the organizational structure that strategically align with the size of franchise system. The arrangement of organizational structure also depends upon the products and services provided by the franchisees and the overall franchise business model. For example, because a fast-food franchise is among the most complex and unique franchise structures based upon menu creation, product procurement, and operating system requirements franchisors in this sector will need to employ corporate staff with an expertise in food preparation, ingredients, and product sourcing. These positions require individuals that can create new menu items, are aware of where to purchase ingredients, and can participate in the creation of training regimes for franchisees and their employees.

To create the proper organizational structure, franchisors need to incorporate their organization size and the number of operating locations into their decision-making. The organizational structure would need to be updated when the existing structure no longer supports the growth of franchisee units. If the existing company operation consists of a few locations, as the franchise system grows the franchisor will transition from a smaller franchisor organization into a larger one that is commensurate with the increasing growth responsibilities of franchisor staff that may need to be specialized. While we will focus on a startup franchisor organizational structure in this chapter, in this section, we provide three sample organizational structures to illustrate how these structures differ for franchise startups, typically up to 25 franchised locations, a mid-size franchise with 50–100 locations, and a more established franchise brand that exceed over 100 locations.

Figure 6.1 presents the organizational structure of a franchise startup that delineates the key positions and staff. Although there may be variations among franchisor startup organizational structures, the core feature is its simplicity and flat hierarchy because the franchise system has not been developed and only requires minimal staff. Also, because most franchise startups emerge from small companies, there is a lack of

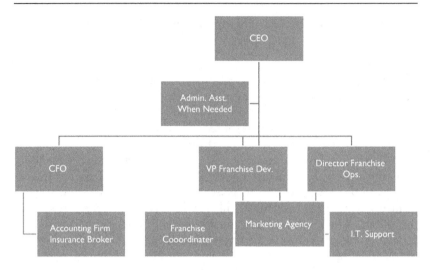

Figure 6.1 A Tradional Franchisor Startup.

capital to fund a more robust franchisor organization and several TMT often needs to be responsible for diverse tasks and groups from multiple functional areas. In most cases, the franchisor startup would often choose to outsource certain functions, such as Marketing and IT Support services, that are less vital to the core franchise business until the franchise system reaches it next stage of development.

Figure 6.2 presents an example of the organizational structure for a typical mid-sized franchisor that administers a network of 50–100 franchise locations. This figure illustrates that the TMT has been expanded to include a Chief Operating Officer (COO), and VP Operations support staff. To support and manage the growth and development of the franchise network, mid-size franchisors often need to hire additional franchise development staff, a Marketing Director, and IT Manager. In addition, field staffs who can train, support, and audit new franchisees are important human capital to acquire.

To support the responsibilities of the CFO in managing increasingly complex financial resources, additional staff would be added, including an accounting manager, accounts receivable, and accounts payable positions. Finally, for a mid-sized franchisor who intends to expand internationally, it would require the franchisor to recruit and assign the responsibility for international operations to a dedicated franchise operations staff member. Overall, the organizational structure of a mid-sized franchisor would be more complicated and hierarchical, compared with that of a franchise startup.

Figure 6.3 depicts the structure of an established mature franchisor which can have from 100 to 500 or more franchise locations. When a

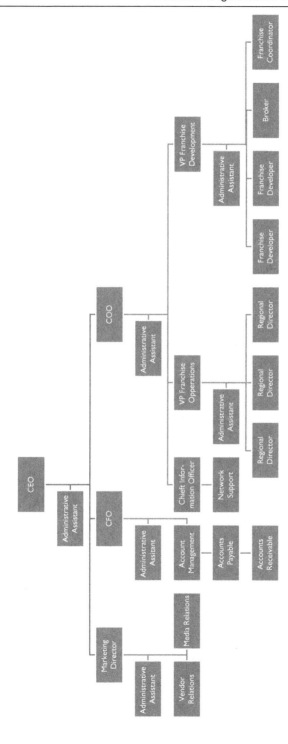

Figure 6.2 A Mid-Size Franchise System.

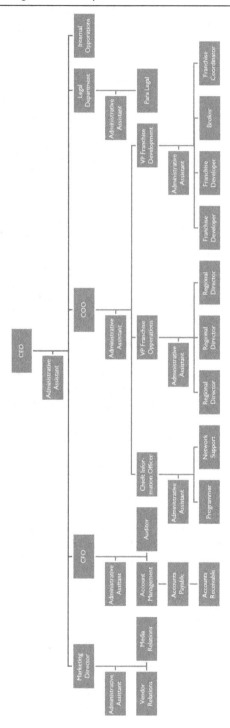

Figure 6.3 A Mature Franchise System.

franchise system reaches this size, the franchisor will require extensive staff to support the TMT, which can include a National Accounts Director who would implement and administer National Accounts, an auditor who would audit franchisor and franchisee financial transactions when appropriate.

There should be additional marketing staff to support advertising, promotional programs, and expenditures from the advertising fund as marketing strategies need to strike a balance between globalization and localization approaches.[2] Those franchisors with several hundred franchise locations may have an in-house legal department and where appropriate VP of International Operations. To resolve these complex and unique issues that large franchisors often encounter, their organizational structure tends to be highly complex, hierarchical, and rigid with individual employees specializing on few tasks within a specific functional area and TMT mainly overseeing the overall strategic directions of the firm.

Top Management Team

The development of organization capability begins by understanding the key top management team (TMT) members of the franchise system that are essential for launching and building the new franchise operation. With this understanding, franchisors could then effectively identify and recruit the right candidates for these positions. The main source of the TMT members could come from the existing company operation.

In many cases, certain franchisor TMT positions can be filled by existing company executives, such as the Chief Executive Officer (CEO), Chief Financial Officer (CFO), and a Franchise Coordinator. Other top management positions, such as the Vice President of Franchise Development and Director of Franchise Operations should ideally be recruited externally as these positions would benefit from hiring individuals with prior franchise experience. Further, at the early startup stage of franchise system development, especially when human capital is limited, some franchisor top management team members could take on the responsibilities of another vacant TMT position. For example, a franchise startup will not require a full-time Training Director, so the key responsibility of this position, such as franchisee training and development, could be fulfilled by the Director of Franchise Operations or even the CEO. Alternatively, if a vacant TMT position could not be filled by the existing company executives or managers, then franchisors would need to recruit and identify external candidates with the proper knowledge, skills, capabilities, and franchise experience. Indeed, this external search is quite common especially when franchise systems are going through a rapid development stage.

According to Doug Kushell, the founder of Franchise Search, who has been placing franchise industry talent in key positions, including CEO,

COO, Franchise Operations, and International Development, for over three decades, it is common for franchisors to work with executive recruiters who specialize in the franchise industry to identify the best candidates for vacant TMT positions. He indicated that the most frequent search positions for emerging franchisors are for Franchise Development followed by Franchise Operations. These executive recruiters could sometimes recruit individuals who have worked for other related stakeholders, such as franchisor suppliers, to fill the vacant positions because they have experience interacting with franchisors and franchisees. This provides them an understanding of the franchise business model, and some may have an existing relationship with the franchisor staff or the franchisees which could enable their performance.

Whatever the source of franchisor human capital whether from in-house company staff, recruiters, or existing relationships it is important that the most qualified and capable staff be in place because they will be responsible to the franchisor but also its franchisees who have a financial interest in the success of the franchise. Next, we discuss these key positions and their key responsibilities in the order of.

Chief Executive Officer

The Chief Executive Officer (CEO) is the person responsible for directing and leading the franchisor organization. Table 6.1 highlights the CEO's key responsibilities. The role of the CEO grows in importance as the franchise system evolves into a larger company, however, regardless of franchise system size, this position is critical to the success of the franchise. This person will be responsible for the overall operation of the franchise, providing its vision, establishing key objectives, and capable of guiding the franchisor TMT and the franchisees to fulfill their collective goals.

The CEO will establish and approve the major objectives of key franchisor staff to include the number of new franchisees, the addition of new products or services, and major advertising campaigns. An effective franchisor CEO should demonstrate their creative abilities when structuring the franchise program in concert with their franchise advisors. The CEO must focus on building a franchise brand while ensuring that the initial franchisees are satisfied. This is a very challenging aspect of building and cultivating a new franchise system which is one of the important responsibilities of the CEO.[3]

The most successful franchisor founders and CEOs, including Ray Kroc of McDonald's, Dave Thomas of Wendy's, Fred Deluca of Subway, and Peter Cancro who founded the highly successful Jersey Mikes franchise, were entrepreneurs who focused upon activities that helped propel the growth of their franchise brand and their relationship with franchisees. They actively participated in the development of their

Table 6.1 CEO Responsibilities

Chief Executive Officer	
Franchise Leadership	The franchisor CEO must guide the franchisor organization through the franchise launch, startup phase including qualifying and appointing key franchisor staff. This is important because this person is the leader of the franchise and someone who franchisees look to for direction, guidance, and support.
Franchise System Growth	Establishing short- and long-term franchise development objectives. Determine the appropriate targets for new franchisee growth in coordination with VP Franchise Development. This is key for the franchisor to have consistent new franchisee development and drive franchisee recruitment, presentation, and sales strategies.
Franchisor Representative	Serve as the primary spokesperson for the franchise brand in recruitment advertising, with the media, industry representatives and franchise trade associations. As the face of the franchise brand, there must be a consistent image and voice.
Establishing Financial and Operating Objectives	Coordinate objectives with financial and operating management to establish targets that are shared throughout the franchisor organization. Without clearly defined financial and operating objectives the franchisor can lack a consistent strategy employed by components of the franchisor staff.
Franchise Relationship Management	Has key responsibility for overseeing the state of franchise relations between the franchisor and franchisees using satisfaction surveys and franchisee feedback to identify franchisee satisfaction levels. Positive franchise relations are an attribute of successful franchise systems.

franchise system, played an active role in interacting with their franchisees, and became the voice and face of their franchise brand. Each was innovative and implemented programs and strategies that were used by other franchisors.

This is one of the major traits that sets successful franchise CEOs apart from company CEOs who are engaged to lead an existing company and tend to have administrative and management responsibilities and unlike franchisor CEOs, are not accountable to franchisee owner-operators. Because a franchisor CEO is dealing with franchisees who made an investment in a franchise compared to company employees the CEO must be able to lead an organization that reflects this distinction.

Because most startup franchisors emerge from small businesses, it is not uncommon for startup franchisors who develop into larger organizations to recruit a CEO with experience operating large franchisors because the founder/CEO may have some limitations operating a large franchisor. In these cases, the founder may assume the title of President leaving the CEO responsible for leading the day-to-day operation of the franchise.

An effective CEO must have the ability to relate to franchisees during the pre- and post-franchise startup phase. They must be capable of promoting the franchise brand and establishing the corporate culture of the franchisor because they will be the voice of the franchise. Eddy Goldberg of Franchise Update Media Group interviewed seven franchisor CEOs who collectively represented 4,600 franchise locations. They were asked to present their key roles and areas of concern as the CEO and leader of their franchise. The most prominent mentions by these CEOs included recruiting franchisees and training those franchisees and trainers, to maintain an active role in their operations. Focusing on franchise system growth and prosperity, growing existing franchisee sales and profits, and listening to their franchisees. Finally, they were the face of the organization and set and communicated the mission and vision for the franchise network for current times and five or more years ahead.

Chief Financial Officer

The Chief Financial Officer (CFO) will report to the CEO and occupy a strategic role in the overall leadership of the franchisor. Table 6.2 lists the CFO's key responsibilities. The CFO may already occupy a position in the company, but previous franchise experience is not a requirement for this position.

Barry Knepper, CPA, who operates the Franchise CPA, provides financial statements and royalty audits to emerging and mid-size franchisors. He states that if you are a small to mid-sized franchisor, having a CFO is important so that one person is focused on creating long and short-term financial goals, obtaining financing, improving profitability, and ensuring financial information is timely and accurate. If a startup franchisor cannot afford or justify a full-time CFO at the early startup stage a part-time CFO can fulfill the requirements and necessary results. According to Knepper, it is the responsibility of the CFO to establish the franchisor Chart of Accounts to organize transactions and provide inputs to the financial statements. If the Chart of Accounts is not properly set-up it, it can result in errors and misinformation in the franchisor's financial statements. Because franchisors collect franchise and advertising fees from their franchisees these funds must be properly accounted

Table 6.2 CFO Responsibilities

Chief Financial Officer	
Financial Accounts, System Controls, and Capital Flow	Establish the required accounts, financial systems, and controls necessary to produce financial statements and protect the financial assets of the franchisor. Manage and control the financial-related activities of the franchisor including accounting, payroll, financial planning and analysis, billing and collections, and accounts payable. Monitor and maintain capital availability and where required source additional funds.
Financial Controls	The CFO has the obligation for implementing and maintaining the franchisor controls, and the accounts of royalty and continuing payments. This is an important requirement for protecting the assets and revenues of the franchisor.
Preparing and Tracking Budgets	Responsible for budgets, ensure that effective internal controls are in place and maintain compliance with GAAP and applicable federal, State, and local regulatory laws and rules for financial and tax reporting. Provide input to the marketing department when considering possible franchise price promotion programs.
Franchisee Performance Reports and Analysis	The CFO will be responsible for monitoring the financial performance of franchisees by compiling data from franchisee financial statements and publishing results to appropriate franchisor staff. They will also be responsible for establishing Key Performance Indicators which can be used to monitor franchisee performance utilizing key data points. These are necessary requirements for identifying how the franchisees perform.
Maintaining Insurance Coverage for the Franchisor	The CFO works with a qualified insurance agent to ensure that the proper franchisor coverages are in place. They must obtain the proper coverages for the franchisor and ensure that franchisees comply with the required insurance coverages stipulated in their franchise agreements.

for and must be disclosed in the franchisor FDD. There may be a need to account for purchases made by franchisees from required franchisor vendors and any rebates received by the franchisor, all of which must be disclosed in the FDD.

A CFO should have a deep understanding of the franchise business model and banking relationships and may work with the board of directors. The CFO prepares detailed financial and management reports, works with auditors, oversees tax planning, and sets policies around controls and payroll. Their responsibilities include budgeting and forecasting, managing mergers or acquisitions, and compliance issues.

The CFO should be forward-thinking as they consider economic, industry, tax, government regulation, and social issues. A CFO is especially valuable for a company that is growing quickly, has many employees, and has complex product lines. Finance officers also bring tremendous value to a company when it is considering acquiring or preparing itself to be acquired.[4]

Vice President Franchise Development

The Vice President (VP) Franchise Development is responsible for administering the franchise department and directing the recruitment, qualifications, document distribution, and is the primary contact for qualified franchise candidates. Table 6.3 highlights the key tasks of a VP. This person reports to the CEO and is a key member of the TMT. They are responsible for managing the Franchise Coordinator to ensure that franchise leads are being properly processed and recorded and franchise program materials are forwarded to the candidate. They should have experience with all components of the franchising process from recruiting candidates to completing franchise transactions.

The VP Franchise Development plays an important role in leading the development, growth, and success of the franchise program. This person has the key responsibility of guiding people through the franchise process. If the VP fails to properly execute its responsibilities, it will have a significant impact on the ability of the franchisor to effectively fund the franchise operation and even achieve success due to a lack of franchise fees and royalties. They will be responsible for helping to structure franchisee presentations by members of the TMT.

In some startup franchise programs, this position is filled on a temporary basis by the franchisor CEO because it can enable them to learn about the franchise recruitment and development process before adding a person to fill this role. However, if this approach is employed it should be on a short-term basis because there are important responsibilities associated with this position.

Table 6.3 VP Franchise Development Responsibilities

Vice President (VP) Franchise Development	
Franchise system growth	Constructing franchisee system growth projections and submitting to the CEO for approval. At the initial startup stage, this is an important component of the franchisor budgeting process because franchisees are the only way to generate franchisor revenues.
Franchisee recruitment and lead generation	Design and implement franchisee recruiting programs, monitor and evaluate the results of franchisee recruitment programs and supervise the intake, approval, and documentation of all franchise inquires. This is an important activity because the goal is to maximize franchisee leads at the most reasonable cost.
Franchisee Prospects Qualifications	Review and approve franchisee applications, engage with qualified franchise candidates, and at early franchise stage guide candidates through the franchising process. This is an important role of the VP because qualifying franchise prospects is a key component of the franchising process.
Franchise Regulatory Compliance	The VP is responsible for complying with franchise offering and sales regulations per regulatory requirements of the FTC and in any States where the franchisor can sell franchises. It is important that all franchise development activities comply with all franchise regulatory requirements and are properly documented.
Franchisee Negotiations	Participate with franchisor attorney in contract negotiations with franchise candidate and their attorney. Interface with franchisor field operations to be aware of franchisee performance issues and assist franchise operations with franchisee relationship management when appropriate.
Franchise Documentation	Administers staff responsible for fulfilling franchise documentation requirements to include maintaining and filing franchisee contractual documents, franchisor–franchisee communications, agreements, and related information.

Franchise Coordinator

The Franchise Coordinator (FC) reports to the VP Franchise Development and plays an important role in franchise development because the FC is typically the first person from the franchisor's staff a potential franchisee speaks with. They frequently communicate with franchise prospects as the prospect moves through the franchising process. It is important that the FC creates a favorable impression on behalf of the franchisor because they communicate with many potential franchisees some on a continuing basis.

The FC is responsible for sending franchise information and FDDs to qualified franchise prospects and will support the VP Franchise Development and development staff throughout the franchising process. Previous experience interacting with customers in a customer service, telemarketing, or personnel recruitment environment is an important prerequisite for this position. The FC should have excellent oral and written communication skills and be proficient in MS Word and Excel.

Table 6.4 Franchise Coordinator Responsibilities

Franchise Coordinator	
Franchise lead intake	Responsible for receiving franchise inquiries and recording key prospect information. Answer basic franchise-related questions from individuals when required.
Communicating Franchise Information	Forwarding franchise information, applications, and Franchise Disclosure Documents (FDD) to qualified franchise prospects.
Recording and maintaining franchise documents	Responsible for the tracking, receipt, and filing of all FDD acknowledgment of receipts from franchise prospects.
Contact Franchisee prospects	Interface with franchisee prospects and qualified franchisee candidates from time to time regarding requests, documentation, and on behalf of the VP Franchise Development

Director of Franchise Operations

The Director of Franchise Operations (DFO) will report to the CEO and is responsible for franchisee compliance, diagnosing, and assisting with franchisee operational problems, and conducting franchise compliance audits. Table 6.4 illustrates its key responsibilities. This position may assist franchisees with recruiting and evaluating key franchisee employee candidates. They will assist in franchisee training program presentations. As the franchise grows into a larger franchise system the DFO position can expand into a VP of Franchise Operations or Chief Operating Officer role.

The DFO occupies an important position in the franchisor TMT as the individual will be required to support and assist franchisees in the operation of their franchise. Because successful franchisees are the cornerstone of a successful franchise brand, franchisee support is a key franchisor's responsibility. This individual should be capable of managing a team of franchise field consultants and should have previous management experience. It is vital that this individual have excellent communication skills. As First Author who has served as VP Franchise Operations and COO in both small and large franchise systems, I can attest to the important role this position plays in a franchisor organization. There is responsibility and involvement in virtually every aspect of the franchise operation which requires an individual with a broad range of skills.

The Director of Franchise Operations should coordinate the method and frequency of support the franchisees can expect to receive. Although the franchise agreement will describe the obligations of the franchisor regarding franchisee site visits, grand opening support, and other types of assistance, these are often defined in broad terms. Because franchise candidates may want to know what kind of support, they could expect to receive if they became a franchisee and current franchisees may request support it is important that they receive a consistent response.

As the leader of franchise operations, it's important that this individual has specific skills that will make them an effective franchisor representative who can help franchisees become successful. Franchise operations play an important role in the franchisor organization because it touches on every aspect of franchising and is directly involved with franchisees personally and through subordinates (Table 6.5).

Franchisor Outsourced Services

Depending upon its size and maturity stage, a startup franchisor may require outside support to perform and fulfill certain functions namely, marketing services and information technology (IT) support until the franchise system grows to a certain size. Approximately 70% of startup franchisors are small firms with one or two locations. These startups often do not have dedicated marketing and IT departments and must strategically secure outsourcing companies to provide these services until they reach a certain organizational size. Further, regardless of firm size, franchise companies are required to hire an independent accounting firm to perform annual franchisor financial audits due to regulatory requirements by the Federal Trade Commission and certain states regulations. Next, we highlight three important functional areas that franchise startups often need to seek outsourcing services.

Marketing Agency

Except in rare cases, startup franchisors outsource marketing services until the franchise system reaches a certain number of franchisees. The benefit of outsourcing is to control operating expenses by spending on marketing programs when needed. Marketing is an important activity for a franchisor because it's needed to create marking materials, establish

Table 6.5 Director of Franchise Operations Responsibilities

Director of Franchise Operations	
Franchisee Training	Administer franchisee training and assist in initial franchisee training to properly prepare each franchisee to operate their franchise. It is important that the DFO or similar position supervise and have a role in franchisee training because they are the most involved franchisor TMT in franchisee operations and have franchisee operating experience.
New franchise opening assistance	Provide franchisee onsite assistance including franchise pre-opening and grand opening assistance and support. Be available for post-opening support if required. This is an important requirement for a successful franchisee startup.
Franchisee support	Provide franchisee support where required and needed to assist franchisees who are underperforming. At the initial stage of franchise operations, the DFO may provide direct assistance to franchisees, and as the number of franchise locations increases, field staff may be added to support the DFO in providing franchisees assistance and to perform audits.
Franchisee Compliance	The DFO and staff will perform site visits to ensure franchisee compliance with required franchise operating procedures. Except for non-retail franchises where consumers are not attending the location it is important that franchise sites be audited to validate compliance. These audits are necessary to uphold proper and consistent franchise standards.
Marketing Support	They will assist franchisees in local marketing and promotional program design and execution. This is important because franchise performance will depend in part upon local marketing. The DFOs can use their marketing experience with other franchisees to transfer this knowledge to new franchisees.
Franchise Development	The DFO will participate in certain franchise development presentations including Discovery Day to provide details regarding franchisor training and support. As prospective franchisees will seek validation of franchisor support from the franchisor and existing franchisees, it is important that the DFO participate in the franchise development process.
Franchise Relations	Assist with franchisor disputes and franchise relation issues from time to time.

promotional programs, and assist in the introduction of new products or services. A common tactic is for a startup franchisor to outsource its marketing activities to create marketing materials, assist in the website design and construct a grand opening program for its new franchisees. The marketing firm can also provide input to the franchisor regarding other marketing activities on an as-needed basis. The marketing firm will support the VP of Franchise Development in the design and placement of franchisee recruiting ads. The firm also works closely with the Director of Franchise Operations in the design and placement of franchisee promotional advertising.

IT Support

It is unusual for a small company or startup franchisor to have an IT Department and like most small companies will usually outsource IT support and assistance. Whether there is an existing IT staff member or it is necessary to go outside the organization, it is important to have this resource available because the franchisor and its franchisees will require support from time to time. This function will report to the Director of Franchise Operations because it will help to implement various software programs used by franchisees and may provide email addresses and Social Media sites for franchisees. Electronic reporting, franchisor financial reports, and required franchise software may require intervention by IT support to help or in case of problems. For example, to download specific information from franchisees may require IT support to effectuate the most efficient method.

Independent Accounting Firm

An independent accounting firm is required to assist the franchisors to prepare audited financial statements to be included in the FDD. The Federal Trade Commission and certain states require a franchisor to have financial statements prepared each year and the statements must be included as an exhibit to the updated FDD. A new franchisor is permitted in most states to "phase-in" the preparation and disclosure of audited financials over an initial 2-year period. This means that a new franchisor may not need an audit in the first year of operation but will need an audited balance sheet in year two and a full audit by year three of operation. It is important for a new franchise system to engage early with a CPA firm that can audit the business and become familiar with the disclosure requirements of franchise systems under state and federal law. Financial statements are required in several franchise-related documents, such as the FDD and Franchise Business Plan. The accounting firm will work closely with the CFO and CEO.

Summary

In this chapter, we discussed the importance of establishing the franchisor's organizational structure and key positions that play a key role in the startup organization. We refer to this important group of executives and managers as the franchisor Top Management Team or TMT. Beginning with the Chief Executive Officer each position is described including the key responsibilities and qualifications. Each of these positions including the CEO, CFO, VP Franchise Development, and Director of Franchise Operations, collectively play a major role in launching the new franchise operation.

We explain that certain functions such as marketing and IT services may be outsourced to outside firms until the franchisor achieves a certain size. Finally, although most startup franchisors start with a small group of executives some franchisors can startup with the capital that can enable them to launch their franchise with a more robust TMT and staff. As a franchise system develops into more franchise locations, the franchisor will add more staff to complement and perform its key duties and responsibilities pertaining to its franchisees.

Notes

1 Chadwick, C., Super, J. F., & Kwon, K. (2015). Resource orchestration in practice: CEO emphasis on SHRM, commitment-based HR systems, and firm performance. *Strategic Management Journal*, 36(3), 360–376. Scott, W. R. (1975). Organizational structure. *Annual Review of Sociology*, 1(1), 1–20.
2 Jain, S. C. (1989). Standardization of international marketing strategy: Some research hypotheses. *Journal of Marketing*, 53(1), 70–79. Ramarapu, S., Timmerman, J. E., & Ramarapu, N. (1999). Choosing between globalization and localization as a strategic thrust for your international marketing effort. *Journal of Marketing Theory and Practice*, 7(2), 97–105.
3 Vernon, S. C. (2016). *From Small Business Owner to Franchise CEO: Expanding the Brand While Keeping the Pulse of Day-to-Day Operations*. https://www.franchise.org/franchise-information/franchise-relations/from-small-business-owner-to-franchise-ceo-expanding-the
4 Stowe, S. (2015). Role of the CFO in today's franchise environment. *Inside Franchise Business*. https://www.franchisebusiness.com.au/what-is-the-role-of-a-cfo-in-todays-franchising-environment/

Chapter 7

Franchise System Development

In Chapter 6, we presented three potential organizational structures and delineated essential human resources for franchisors to effectively operate and manage their franchise development program. Once the structure has been implemented, franchisors can begin to promote and develop their franchise. We now move on to discuss Franchise Development which consists of recruiting, selecting, processing, and qualifying franchisee candidates. It is one of the most important activities franchisors engage in because such development enables franchisors to attract highly qualified franchisees to their network and achieve a higher franchisee success rate. The failure of developing successful franchisees can result in the diminishing financial success of franchise performance, and shortfalls in franchisor royalty revenues for the franchisor. Overall, effective franchise development would enable franchisors to finance and grow their franchise organization, build franchise brand recognition and add value to both the franchise and franchisee.

In this chapter, we will discuss how to implement and execute a successful franchise development program following seven sequential steps (Figure 7.1). This franchise development process begins with targeting franchise territories which is essential for implementing a successful franchise development strategy. With target territories identified, it's vital to build a franchisee profile that will be used to recruit and qualify the right franchise candidates. We then discuss the importance for franchisor representatives to properly engage with qualified candidates and effectively address their requests to negotiate the terms of the franchise agreement to complete a franchise transaction. We conclude with a brief description of International Franchising.

Target Franchise Territories

The first step in the franchise development process is identifying the specific franchise territories that would provide the highest demand for the franchise products or services. Targeting franchise territories is a

DOI: 10.4324/9781003034285-7

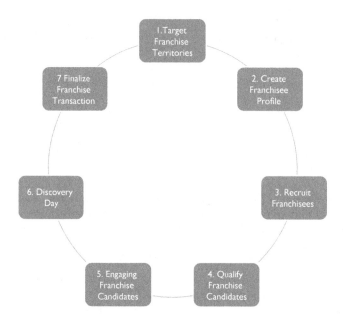

Figure 7.1 The Franchising Development Process.

process based upon careful research instead of intuitive speculation. Key considerations should provide the franchisee a route to profitability by identifying the territory demographics that pertain to the number of potential franchise consumers. For example, a home care franchisor may define a territory of potential consumers by using the number of residents over 65 on Medicare to estimate how many could afford to pay out of pocket for home care services.

In addition, franchisors should also consider various cost aspects of potential territories. For example, if the costs for retail and office space are unusually high, it can prevent a franchisee from generating sufficient revenues to overcome their high occupancy costs. Also, the cost of media in a specific territory is an important consideration because high media costs can make promotional advertising costly for the franchisee and franchisor. Despite the large number of potential consumers, certain geographic areas such as Long Island, New York, with costly retail space, labor, and taxes can be an obstacle to some franchises achieving profitability.

One of the best examples of an effective territory development strategy for startup franchisors is the wheel and spoke approach where franchises are granted in concentric territories in proximity to franchisor head-quarters, typically 2–3 hours, drive time. This enables the franchisor to build brand recognition and support its new franchisees. In addition to conducting in-house analysis, franchisors should use a dependable market research firm that applies reliable consumer demographics to identify the most desirable territories to target.

Create the Franchisee Profile

After identifying the territories available for franchisees, the franchisor needs to create an ideal franchisee profile, which helps to identify the most qualified individuals to be recruited as franchisees. A franchisee profile is a set of attributes and qualifications that the ideal franchisee candidate for a particular franchise should possess. In the past, franchise candidates were often evaluated based upon their financial qualifications without considering other factors. In recent years, additional emphasis on qualifying franchise candidates has led to using a more sophisticated franchisee profile. This approach can often improve accuracy and reduce the time and costs to recruit qualified candidates.

A proper franchisee profile consists of several categories of information and its content may vary depending on the industry a franchise system operates in. One set of information that is universal and would enable a franchisor to recruit the best candidates is the desirable knowledge, skills, and abilities of candidates. For example, franchises that provide specialized customer services such as automotive repair services would require a candidate to have pertinent skills and experience.

A franchisee profile should also specify a candidate's minimum financial qualifications, particularly their net worth and available liquid capital. The profile should include a candidate's previous business ownership and accomplishments to confirm that the candidate has specific business experience and skills that would enable them to better operate the franchise. In certain cases, management experience is important for franchise concepts that require the coordinated effort of many employees because a lack of this management experience could hamper a franchisee's potential success.

Another factor that should be included in the franchisee profile is personality characteristics. For example, an extroverted personality may be important for certain franchise business concepts that depend upon direct sales and business-to-business sales activities, such as real estate and business services franchises. Another part of the franchise profile is whether the franchisee has the business experience to operate a single franchise unit versus multiple franchise locations because some franchisors prefer to recruit both single-unit and multi-unit franchisee candidates.

Finally, the timetable for a franchisee to open a franchise is important because it enables franchisors to set priority when identifying and evaluating potential candidates. Often, franchise candidates who prefer to open a franchise unit sooner in the same franchise territory would be more qualified. Some franchisors establish franchise opening timelines based upon the type of franchise that requires a franchisee candidate to open within a specific period. For example, a hotel franchisor may allow more than a year for an opening due to the complexity of the project.

Franchisors should frequently update their franchisee profile to ensure its accuracy and usability. These updates allow franchisors to continue to confirm whether a franchise candidate exhibits the characteristics to launch and operate a successful franchise business. These updates would require the usage of scientific human resource management,[1] such as job analysis and performance evaluation, to improve the predictability of the franchisee profile on future franchisee performance.

Craig Slavin, President/Founder of Franchise Central and the owner of Franchise Navigator, states that understanding and quantifying the skills and the behavioral qualities that a company is seeking can be achieved using a behavioral assessment tool designed for franchise applications. Franchise Navigator, a Skills, Values and Behavioral Assessment, has been used by hundreds of franchisors to model the skills and competencies of an ideal franchise prospect. This can represent the difference between the success or failure of a franchise. A high performer profile is created by benchmarking the performance of existing franchise operators and or unit-level managers. This profile is used to compare inbound candidates to determine whether the candidates have the right credentials to be a franchise operator.

Recruiting Franchise Candidates

Recruiting franchise candidates refers to the process of franchisors utilizing various marketing and advertising techniques to encourage qualified individuals to reach out and apply to be franchise candidates. It is also commonly referred to as franchise lead generation. The franchisee profile will play a key role in determining how and where to recruit franchise candidates. For example, if the franchisee profile requires the prospect to have a financial background, then the best venue to reach potential candidates could be communicating such franchise opportunity on business publications such as *The Wall Street Journal*. Homecare franchisors may choose to advertise in one of the various healthcare publications. Without the ability to generate viable franchise leads, a franchisor cannot grow its franchise system. To effectively recruit candidates, franchisors should prepare and utilize the following toolsets to ensure that potential franchisees understand and appreciate the values of joining their franchise system.

Franchise Marketing Materials

Franchise marketing materials are designed to communicate the features, benefits, and other relevant information of a franchise to its prospective franchisees. It is important for franchisors to carefully craft marketing materials to deliver an effective message to franchise inquiries. Because potential franchisees often obtain and compare franchise information from several franchise opportunities, poorly done marketing materials could be associated with poor franchise opportunities as studies have shown that document readability could easily influence investment decisions.[2]

To construct effective marketing materials, franchisors should review examples of marketing materials from several competitors to identify the typical content and structures they are communicating to potential franchise prospects. These include a description of the franchise, and its market, consumers, benefits, and features. In the franchise description, it also includes the minimum and maximum franchise investment amount. The primary marketing materials used in ads should be available to franchise candidates in a franchise brochure.

Franchisors may email a digital franchise brochure directly to an individual or allow it to be downloaded from the franchise website. Most franchisors use a similar format to describe and present the key attributes of their franchise, except the content varies depending upon the franchise opportunity. If there are no in-house marketing resources available to create the franchisor advertising materials, then a marketing firm should be used for the project.

The Franchise Website

The franchisor needs to build franchise website pages that can present the benefits and features of its franchise opportunity. The franchise website consists of several pages that describe the franchise's products or services, market opportunity, investment requirements, and other pertinent information relating to the franchise. Some franchisors choose to have the franchise pages as a part of the existing website while other franchisors use a separate franchise website that could be accessed from their primary website.

The franchise website pages should include a short information form that the visitor can fill out and submit to download franchise information. The design of the franchise website is important because it will highlight the franchise program which should generate sufficient interest by visitors so they will want to obtain more franchise information. Franchisor, Russo's New York Pizzeria, has a complete website that includes information about the franchise, a history of the company and product information. The Bright Star Home Care franchise uses a website to describe and market its home care services, information presenting its franchise opportunity is opened by clicking a link on their main website.

It is important to utilize the services of an experienced website developer unless existing staff has that capability. Some franchisors prefer to have the franchise pages integrated with the main franchisor customer website. This allows the franchisor to achieve two objectives; present its history, products/services, and relevant information to potential customers and describe the franchise and provide information on the franchise opportunity. The design of the website should create a desire on the part of the visitor to click on the appropriate pages.

An example of an effective franchise website is Kung Fu Tea a Queens, New York based franchisor, advertises as America's largest bubble tea brand with over 250 locations in the United States. It lists some of its services on its franchise pages including site location recommendations, a standard store layout and interior design, and assistance during the franchise grand opening for up to 2 weeks.

Franchise Brokers

Franchise brokers can be an excellent source of franchise candidates. Most franchise brokers are independent contractors who may be affiliated with one or more franchise broker groups. Broker groups have a portfolio of franchisors they represent that can amount to several hundred. The major responsibility of a franchise broker is to present a franchise candidate to a franchisor after fully qualifying the candidate and obtaining a completed franchise application. A major advantage of brokers is that the franchisor does not have to manage them, and a capable broker can qualify the franchise candidate and match them to the most appropriate franchise opportunity. When the candidate is initially presented to the franchisor, they should be vetted as to their qualifications and interest in the franchise. A disadvantage of using a franchise broker is that some may try to shift a franchisee prospect to a franchise brand that provides the broker with a higher commission.

If a broker sells a franchise, they typically receive 50% of the franchise fee as a commission or a minimum amount. Large brokers organizations using brokers generate a high volume of leads from their websites. Franchisors rarely grant exclusivity to one broker organization, which means a franchisor can use several broker groups while still marketing their own franchises. Except for a unique and attractive startup franchise, most brokerage firms will only accept franchisors with a minimum number of locations since there is history of franchisee performance. Franchisors typically use a combination of in-house franchise development staff supplemented by franchise brokers.

Franchise Advertising Portals

Advertising portals are advertising sites that feature franchise opportunities. The cost to advertise on these sites can be on a cost-per-lead basis or a monthly subscription fee. Franchise advertising portals have high visit rates from people interested in franchise opportunities, and visitors can filter franchise opportunities based on business category, investment amount, and available locations. However, although inquiries can be filtered based upon investment and type of franchise several leads from ad portals can be poor. It is important that ad portals are evaluated based upon the number of franchises sold as a percentage of total cost of leads. For example, it's more efficient to sell five franchises for leads that cost $2,000 than to sell two franchises that cost $1,200. The number of franchisor leads will vary depending upon website placement; the more you pay the more leads you are apt to get. The best advertising portals will provide the most qualified leads; therefore, franchisors should seek quality over quantity.

The Internet

The Internet can be a useful source of franchise leads. One way to generate franchise leads on the Internet is accomplished by publishing original content about the franchise in blogs of 300 to 500 words using specific keywords to maximize Search Engine Optimization. To learn which keywords are the best, franchisors can subscribe to Google Ad Words which provides a listing of the most frequently searched keywords. The cost of specific keywords, known as Pay Per Click, will vary depending upon how many times it is searched. For example, the keywords "franchise opportunity" is one of the costliest keywords for a franchisor Internet ad., compared to "franchise attorney."

It is important that franchisors can be easily searchable on the Internet. Using more highly searched keywords in blogs or communication materials would result in a greater opportunity that the franchise will be found via online searches. However, the cost to recruit franchisees on the Internet increases as more money is spent on identifying highly searched keywords. Some franchisors outsource their Internet marketing to companies with an expertise in Search Engine Optimization which can increase franchise website visits.

This approach for recruiting potential franchisees online is often referred as content marketing, i.e., the use of blogs, social media posts, research articles, infographics, and other information relative to a franchise posted on websites, online publications, and franchise sites. Content marketing can be an important source of leads and for directing attention to a franchise website. Blogs can be a productive source of leads because

"Marketers using blogs receive 67% more leads than those who don't use blogs."[3] A number of franchisors use contributors to write blogs that can be posted on the franchisor's website and LinkedIn. These blogs often would be shared on Twitter and/or Facebook. Research articles are often crafted by marketing research firms, which could elicit interest from franchisee prospects.

Franchise Trade Shows

Franchise trade shows are held in certain cities throughout the United States and are used to present and promote franchise opportunities. The most popular franchise trade shows are held by MFV Expositions and sponsored by the International Franchise Association. Participants are limited to franchisors and related vendors and are held in major markets including New York, Nashville, Los Angeles, Miami, and Houston. As exhibiting at a franchise trade show can be costly, it is important that a startup franchisor carefully consider the location, number of estimated visitors, and whether the monies can be used in more effective ways to recruit franchise candidates.

Print Advertising

The use of print media for generating franchise leads has shrunk due to its cost and the dominance of digital media. Most print advertising for franchisee lead gen consists of listings in franchise directories such as *The Franchise Handbook*, *Bonds Franchise Guide,* and the *International Franchise Association Franchise Opportunities Guide* which is for IFA members. Some of these placements are free while others charge a minimal cost. It is important for startup franchisors to post their franchise on these directories because the costs are reasonable and it provides added exposure.

The effectiveness of the above-mentioned toolsets has been documented over the years. One of the key measures is how many franchise candidates are generated from the various recruitment methods and invest in the franchise. The Franconnect Sales Index Webinar Study in 2020 indicated that franchise websites accounted for 28.7% of leads source while franchise ad portals accounted for 9.2% of leads.[4] In addition, a report of franchise sales activity for 2020 from Franconnect revealed that although referrals from brokers are not in the top five sources of leads, they resulted in 20.1% of completed franchise deals. This important metric reveals that the number of quality franchise leads to complete one franchise deal is what truly matters. Broker referrals were 6.6%, while franchise referral consultants and website leads resulted in 4.25% and 1.25%, respectively, of completed deals. Overall, the average percent of leads required to close a franchise deal was found to be 1.07%. These statistics point out the important contribution successful franchisees can make to franchise development and how brokers play a key role in franchise system growth by delivering qualified and fully vetted candidates to the franchisor.

Processing and Qualifying Franchisee Leads

After generating franchise leads, the next step in the franchise development process is processing and qualifying franchisee leads and inquiries from potential franchise candidates. This step refers to the methods and procedures franchisors utilize to identify the most capable and best-qualified franchisees for their franchise system. It consists of a preliminary review of an individual's qualifications followed up by specific candidates completing and submitting a formal franchise application. Regardless of how the franchisor receives a lead, a Franchise Information Form (FIF) needs to be completed by an individual on the franchise website or by the Franchise Coordinator when receiving a telephone inquiry.

It is important to obtain preliminary information on every franchise lead to perform an initial qualification of a candidate by determining whether they have the financial qualifications and are requesting a franchise territory that is available. By having preliminary information pertaining to a franchise lead, it can prevent franchise development staff from devoting their time to unqualified franchise leads. Following is a sample form known as an FIF that can be used or edited for recording basic franchisee information

---

Franchisee Information Form

Name:
Address:
             City: State: Zip:
Telephone:
Email:
Desired Territory:
Amount Available to Invest: Liquid Capital_____   Total Capital_____
Time to Open: 3 months 6 months 1 year.

The most productive way to record and track franchise leads is through Contact Relationship Management (CRM) software which can store and record activities, information and update the status of franchise candidates. With the use of CRM and retained contact information, periodic emails can be sent to people who expressed an initial interest in the franchise. This process is known as a drip campaign. Further, an analysis of the data can help to provide information on the entire franchising process including the source of franchise leads and how long it takes to complete each stage of the franchising process. Franchisors that use a CRM system, should make sure that they have a backup to the system software. Finally, it is important that all paperwork, correspondence, and notes relating to a qualified franchise candidate is in a file under the person's name.

The Franchise Application

Once potential franchisees have been initially qualified, the next step is to have them complete a franchise application. A franchise application consists of several sections requesting information to be furnished by the franchisee prospect. Some franchisors would make their franchise application available on their website, so it is easier for franchise applicants to download, complete, and submit the application at an early stage in the franchise development process.

Because completing a franchise application requires an individual to provide a good deal of personal and financial information, a completed application usually indicates that applicants have a keen interest in the franchise. Based upon assorted industry sources, 10%–15% of franchise candidates who have an approved franchise application and are considered qualified. Franchise brokers who devote considerable time engaging a candidate will judiciously qualify a candidate before presenting them to the franchisor. The broker process can lead to 1 out of 7 applications that result in a completed transaction because a broker wants to be sure that an individual, they submit to the franchisor is well qualified and committed to investing in the franchise.

Once a completed franchise application is received by the Franchise Department, the franchise candidate should be notified by telephone ASAP and told that they will be contacted once the application is reviewed. The next step is for the VP Franchise Development to review the application with a focus on the person's financial qualifications, personal attributes, and business experience. It is common for franchisors to do a credit check on the applicant. The response time for contacting the person is important because franchise candidates respond favorably to a quick response, especially, regarding their application and do not want to wait longer. Assuming that the initial franchise application is approved, additional information regarding the prospect's qualifications may be gathered from subsequent conversations and a franchise candidate corporate visit.

Qualifying the Franchise Candidate

Once a completed franchise application is received, the next step is for the franchisor to evaluate the application to determine the individuals' franchise qualifications. Qualifying the franchise prospect is the process franchisors use for fully approving an individual's qualifications to be granted a franchise.

Qualifying franchise candidates is a vital component of the franchise development process because nothing can be more disruptive and difficult for a franchisor to deal with than a poorly qualified franchisee who cannot properly operate their franchise. When a franchisee fails and is terminated it must be reported on the FDD, which can be harmful to a startup franchisor. Further, a franchisee candidate who is not properly qualified can result in potential problems that can include deficient performance in operating their franchise and in some cases a failed franchise. Poor qualifications can include a franchisee prospect that is undercapitalized which can prevent them from having sufficient capital until the franchise becomes profitable. It is also important to confirm that the franchisee recognizes how much work it takes to build a successful franchise that could be indicated by unrealistic expectations. Finally, some franchisees are uncoachable and fail to follow the franchisor's advice. The Franchise Department should look for indications that a franchise prospect will be compliant and follow the franchisors operating standards. This can require skilled interviewing techniques on the part of franchise development staff.

As the first author who has supervised franchise development personnel, I cannot overemphasize the importance of properly qualifying franchise candidates. Having been personally involved in hundreds of franchisee transactions for both private and publicly traded franchise companies, I can confirm that the structure and emphasis of a franchise company foster the addition of new franchisees. Many franchisor leaders are focused on growing their franchise system, especially if it is a startup or emerging franchise company because it is a basis for publicity and gaining additional revenues. In addition, franchise development staff who usually earn a salary and a commission for each completed franchise transaction are initiative-taking to sell franchises. On certain occasions, they may promote a franchise candidate who may be partially qualified. I have been personally involved in several situations where the CEO suggested I consider approving a franchise candidate who I did not consider fully qualified. In these cases, the franchisees eventually left the system.

The qualifying process usually starts with an initial review of the prospects' application which can be performed by the VP Franchise Development or a member of the development team. It is important that the review of the franchise application focuses on the attributes and skills of the candidate and how they compare to the franchisee profile. To prevent poorly qualified franchise candidates from being accepted, it is important to construct a franchisee approval committee, which can include members of the Top Management Team or several individuals who can objectively evaluate a candidate such as the CFO and human resource director.

When a franchise candidate is deemed qualified, they should be sent a copy of the FDD and told to review the documents and then contact the Franchise Department with any questions. They should also be advised to utilize a franchise attorney to assist with their review. It is important that the Acknowledge of Receipt for the FDD which is contained at the end of the document has been signed by the franchisee and returned to the franchise department. This must be done 14 days before there any monies are paid or agreements signed by the franchise candidate.

In most cases, the franchise candidate will have initial questions after reviewing the FDD. This often takes place before their attorney has reviewed the FDD and presented their findings to their client. After this, the franchise candidate will have additional questions and possible concerns to discuss with the franchisor representative, leading to the next step of the franchise system development process.

Engaging with the Franchise Candidate

Engaging the franchise candidate represents the process whereby a member of the franchise development team can present the franchise candidate with important aspects of the franchise opportunity and acquire more information regarding the candidates. Once prospective franchisees have been qualified and had an opportunity to review the FDD they will be contacted by the VP Franchise Development or other staff members who can guide the candidate through the franchising process. In larger franchise organizations, the person contacting the candidate is usually a franchise development specialist or salesperson. This will be an opportunity to answer any questions the candidate may have after their initial review of the FDD.

The engagement process is a key part of the franchise development because it will allow the franchisor representative to gain insight regarding any concerns a candidate may have regarding the franchise. This can also provide added information regarding a candidate's qualifications, which may not have been observed from the franchise application. It is essential to assign a specific franchise staff to work with a franchise candidate. This could better ensure a smooth communication flow between the franchisor and franchisees and prevent a candidate from receiving mixed responses. This arrangement can create a good relationship between the franchisor representative and the franchise candidate.

After the candidates' questions and their initial concerns have been sufficiently addressed in the engagement process, franchise candidates often would start to negotiate with franchisors and request certain terms of the franchise agreement to be amended, stricken, or altered. This negotiation process could be quite sensitive as a candidate may have received advice from their attorney to request certain terms of the franchise agreement be altered. It also needs to be determined by the franchisor representative how important certain changes are to completing the franchise process. It is not uncommon for a franchisee candidate to state that a certain provision of the franchise agreement if not changed can be a "deal-breaker."

The problem with agreeing to amend certain terms of the franchise agreement is that other franchisees could claim discrimination on the part of the franchisor. Such a claim could entitle a franchisee to receive financial compensation for the same changes they never received. To preempt these potential issues, franchisors could explicitly state that they do not negotiate some terms of the franchise agreement. Based on the first author's experience, when it comes to a qualified franchise candidate requesting a few changes to the franchise agreement that is not of major importance, most franchisors will acquiesce, except for the leading brands with abundant candidates. When the subject of negotiating terms of the franchise agreement is raised by the franchise candidate or their attorney, franchisors should consult with their franchise attorney before responding unless a precedent has been established.

In general, however, there are certain terms in a franchise agreement that is nonnegotiable.

1   Royalty payments and advertising fund fees are franchisee obligations contained in the franchise agreement. These specify a specific amount of these fees that each franchisee is required to pay on a continuing basis. These should not be negotiable for any franchise candidates; else existing franchisees are likely to question why they did not receive this benefit.

2   The Initial Franchise Fee, paid upon the execution of the franchise agreement, should not be changed in general. The only exception is for a franchisor discount granted to veterans under special programs such as the Vetfran program which was introduced by a franchisor a number of years ago and actively promoted by the International Franchise Association.

3   The initial term of the franchise agreement should be fixed for all franchisees. Most franchise agreements specify a 10-year duration with an option to renew for five additional years. The current franchise terms a franchisor provides should remain the same for all franchisees. It is rare but not unusual for a franchisor to change the term of the agreement for a specific franchisee.

4   Default and termination provisions specify the conditions that can cause a franchisee to be placed in default of the agreement which if not cured can lead to the franchise being terminated. Examples of defaults can range from not being open for business as required to operating an unclean location to selling unauthorized products. It is important that default and termination provisions remain the same for all franchisees and not be changed. Otherwise, the franchisor could be accused of discriminatory franchise practices.

5   Additional franchise agreement provisions that should not be changed for the same reasons are nondisclosure and noncompete provisions, legal venue, franchise site-location size, location, and unauthorized décor.

Following are Items that some franchisors may negotiate:

1   Financing of the initial franchise fee over a brief period could enable a highly qualified candidate to pay the initial franchise fee over several payments. There may be a highly qualified franchise candidate who may not meet the financial qualifications but has exemplary credentials. An arrangement to defer a portion of the initial franchisee fee can be granted, however, this should be disclosed in the FDD in likelihood this concession could be granted.

2   Although most franchisors will not change the initial term of the franchise agreement, which is usually 10 years. Some franchisors may agree to add an additional 5-year renewal term if this could help to close the franchise transaction as it is not a major concession.

3   Deferring a portion of royalty or advertising fund fees for the first few months after franchise opening can be granted, providing the franchisee is obligated to fully pay any deferred fees in full. The franchisor should not waive the full payment of these fees.

4   The size of the franchisee territory can be slightly adjusted, provided it does not represent a major departure from the procedure used by the franchisor to define and grant territories. For example, a franchisor that uses zip codes to define a franchise territory coupled with an estimated population size can be altered to grant a franchisee candidate's request so long as the overall territory adheres to the usual policy.

5   A cap or limit of the franchise Personal Guaranty, whereby a franchisor agrees to personally guarantee any financial obligations owed to the franchisor, may be negotiable. A franchise is held in the name of a corporation without a personal guarantee a corporation may lack the funds or assets to meet its financial obligations the franchisor is entitled to. Because some franchise candidates may not want to risk exposing all their assets to a financial judgment, they

would request a dollar cap on the personal guaranty. One solution could be to agree to a cap that represents 5 years estimated future franchisee royalty fees or a set dollar amount.

6   The right of first refusal for adjoining territories that are available is often negotiable. This is often requested by franchisees as a form of protection when they feel that a future neighboring franchisee could drain revenues from their franchise. It is not unusual for startup franchisors to receive this request. Although some franchisors resist granting this request it is not a major concession providing that the franchisee must exercise this right within a brief time frame, for example, 30 days. Additional stipulations can be included that can make it difficult for only the most capable franchisees to exercise this right. A franchisor should not lose a qualified franchise candidate because an existing franchisee with a first right of refusal drags out the process.

7   Various franchisors are willing to grant changes to the Transfer and Assignment section, which defines the time that the franchisor can exercise their right of first refusal if the franchisee has a qualified buyer for their franchise. Given the typical 10-year term of a franchise agreement, some franchisors take the position that the possibility of this becoming a problem is remote and concede to this request. Franchisors can deal with this request by agreeing that the franchisee may be granted additional time to consummate the sale of their franchise subject to the sole discretion of the franchisor.

The Franchise Discovery Day

The sixth step in the franchise development process is Discovery Day, which is the meeting between the franchise candidate and the franchisor at corporate headquarters. Discovery Day can be the first face-to-face meeting between the franchise candidate and franchisor management. It is important because franchisor staff can meet the franchise candidate, review their qualifications, and make a final informed decision regarding the candidate becoming a franchisee. This is also the last opportunity for the franchisor to confirm that the candidate is qualified. Thus, it is not surprising that every franchisor requires prospective franchisees to visit their corporate headquarters as the last requirement before finalizing the franchise transaction.

The objective of Discovery Day is for franchisor staff to meet the franchise candidate after the candidate has spoken to franchisees, reviewed the FDD, and has gained an understanding of the franchise program. It is also an opportunity for the franchisee candidate to meet franchisor executives, observe the franchisor's corporate culture, obtain answers to any remaining questions, and negotiate any open items pertaining to the franchise agreement. The Franchisor should share the agenda for a Discovery Day visit including a list of attendees with the candidate before the meeting. Although a candidate is responsible for the expenses incurred to attend Discovery Day, some franchisors refund those expenses if the franchisee purchases the franchise.

Franchisors should take a balanced approach to Discovery Day with the following objectives:

1   Provide useful information to the candidate and answer questions.
2   Evaluate and qualify the franchise candidate by obtaining objective feedback from several members of the franchisor staff.
3   Resolve any open issues or concerns on the part of both parties.

If these objectives are fulfilled, then both parties will benefit from Discovery Day and move on to finalize the franchise transaction.

Finalizing the Franchise Transaction

The last step in concluding the franchise transaction is preparing the franchise documents and scheduling a closing date. It is important that all the documents are carefully reviewed by the franchisor before the closing. This should be done to avoid any mistakes like excluding ancillary agreements including the personal guaranty, noncompete, and nondisclosure agreements.

Finalizing the franchise transaction consists of the franchisor preparing all the franchise document, ancillary agreements, and amendments that may reflect any negotiated changes to the franchise agreement and resolving any items that the franchisee candidate or their attorney wish to negotiate. The franchisor should have two people review the documents before presenting them to the franchisee for execution. Relying solely on a franchise development staff member to review the documents can be a mistake because they could miss something. As the first author, we had a franchisee's personal guaranty excluded by the judge in a lawsuit because the franchisee signed the guarantee in the name of their corporation. This meant that the franchisee was not personally liable for the obligations owing to us after the judgment and their corporation had little assets.

Some franchisees may consider the signing of the franchise documents so important they would prefer to execute the documents in person with the franchisor. In some franchise systems, there may be an actual closing where all signatories are in attendance although in current times most franchise documents are signed offsite and originals exchanged.

International Franchising

International franchising takes place when a franchisor decides to grant to another entity, defined as the franchisee, the rights to operate in another country utilizing the franchise brand, trademarks, franchisors system, knowhow, and operating systems. The foreign franchisee pays an initial franchise fee and ongoing royalty fees. It agrees to operate the franchise according to the franchisor obligations contained in an international franchise agreement. Many of the major franchise brands operating in the United States franchise throughout the world.

Countries that have the largest number of franchise brands include the United States, China, India, Brazil, Germany, France, Australia, Japan, and Canada. The popularity and growth of international franchising are evidenced by the World Franchise Council (WFC) which consists of franchise associations from 40 countries. International franchise attorney Carl Zwisler advises that franchisors and potential franchisee candidates should research the market and test the viability of the concept through modeling, using the best available information for each market when developing a plan for that specific market.

Possessing the experience to enter other countries requires that a franchisor has a minimum of 30–50 franchise units, operates a successful franchise brand, and possesses the necessary human and financial capital. Franchisors that consider franchising in other countries should first gain a full understanding of international franchising. Information is available from the U.S. Commercial Service and International Franchise Association. International franchise attorney Carl Zwisler advises that franchisors and potential franchisee candidates should research the market and test the viability of the concept through modeling, using the best available information for each market when developing a plan for that specific market.

Summary

This chapter illustrated the franchise development process, which enables franchisors to build a successful franchise system. The franchise development process is the engine that can propel the growth of a franchise system. We explained that the foundation of a successful franchise development strategy begins by identifying the markets you should target for franchises and profiling the key characteristics of a franchisee candidate. We presented the ways that franchisors recruit franchise candidates and the importance of using CRM software to process franchise leads. We also discussed the significance of properly qualifying a franchise candidate and defined and presented the engagement and negotiation between the franchise candidate and franchisor. This process is then completed with the franchisee candidate Discovery Day.

Notes

1 Cascio, W. (2021). *Managing Human Resources*. McGraw-Hill US Higher Ed USE.
2 Chan, C. R., Park, H. D., Huang, J. Y., & Parhankangas, A. (2020). Less is more? Evidence for a curvilinear relationship between readability and screening evaluations across pitch competition and crowdfunding contexts. *Journal of Business Venturing Insights*, *14*, e00176.
3 Hodge C, Oppewal H., & Terawatanavong, C. (2013). Winmark Franchise Partners (2017). The top elements of a franchise development strategy for emerging franchisors. *European Journal of Marketing*.
4 Gerson, K. (2020). *Franconnect 2020 Franchise Sales Index Webinar*.

Chapter 8

Franchisor Support and Services

In Chapter 7, we presented the components of franchise development and how to recruit, qualify, and engage franchise prospects to complete a franchise transaction. After the franchise agreement is signed and the initial franchise fee paid, the contractual relationship between the franchisor and franchisee begins.

To facilitate the symbiotic relationship between franchisees and franchisors, this chapter illustrates the important toolset, i.e., the franchisor support and services, created by franchisors to better guide and develop their franchisees as it would make the difference between a successful or unsuccessful franchise program. Franchisor support consists of the contractual obligations that franchisors must provide to its franchisees while franchisor services are programs that can facilitate a more successful franchise operation.

Although both parties have specific obligations intended to achieve a successful operation, franchisor support and services is the most important obligation. Because most new franchisees are inexperienced and have not developed an understanding of their roles and tasks in the franchise system, they depend heavily on their franchisors' guidance, and welcome their advice.[1]

Franchisor support includes franchisee training, startup and ongoing franchisee support, specific services, and marketing programs that can help franchisees generate additional revenues and profits. Franchisor services consists of various items which typically include outside IT support, product discounts, supplier purchase discounts, payroll processing, and human resource support. We elaborate the most important components of franchisor support and how these contribute to a successful franchise program. We conclude with a discussion on how to monitor franchisee performance using key performance indicators (KPIs) to ascertain how franchisees are performing and which franchisees may require franchisor advice and assistance.

DOI: 10.4324/9781003034285-8

The Importance of Franchisor Support

As presented earlier, franchise support consists of those contractual obligations that the franchisor is required to provide its franchisees. These items can include site location visits, training, marketing assistance, and marketing programs. Some franchisor support activities may be stated as optional in the franchise agreement. It is important for franchisors to recognize the value of franchisor support and how it can facilitate the franchise development process. People invest in a franchise to build and operate their own business with the expectation that franchisors would provide the training, support, and structure needed to successfully operate their business. The expertise and experience of a franchisor is part of the value that franchisees expect to receive. When a franchisor fails to fulfil the expectations of its franchisee, it can result in various negative consequences.

When a franchisor fails to properly support its franchisees, it can leave some franchises adrift which can lead to mediocre or poor franchise performance. In addition, insufficient franchisor support can prompt a franchisee to request additional operational assistance which would place an additional burden on franchisor resources, that could result in a lack of overall franchisee support.[2] Such a lack of support could result in the failure of franchisees. Given franchise prospects seek positive validation from existing franchisees, the frequent dissatisfaction or even failures of franchisees could lead to serious litigation and make it difficult to convince future franchise prospects to invest in the franchise.

Appropriate franchisor support is needed to ensure that franchisees would have sufficient resources to manage a successful franchise unit. Each component of franchisor support is individually and collectively important. Based on our experience, we have found that the most successful franchise brands deliver substantial franchisee support for all components of franchise operations. This pattern is also observed from a report from Franchise Business Review and InGage Consulting, illustrating the impacts of these franchisor service and support engagements being material and quantifiable. With a sample of 300 brands and 24,000 participants, this study found that franchisees that receive support and are engaged with franchisees are 3.7 times more profitable than franchisees that do not receive active support.[3]

Next, we discuss several key components that are required to grow a new franchisee unit into a successful one. These components include pre-opening assistance, franchise opening assistance, marketing programs, operational support, measuring franchisee financial performance, and franchisee counselling.

Pre-opening Assistance

Pre-opening assistance refers to a set of franchisor activities that will effectively prepare a franchisee for launching their new franchise business. This assistance typically includes site-selection assistance, franchisee training, and franchisor services.

The pre-opening assistance is important because it would prepare the franchisee for finding the right location, understanding the fundamentals of franchise operations, and arranging for the operational services that the franchisor provides. When a franchisor does not provide adequate pre-opening assistance, a franchisee often makes biased decisions. that could impair the performance of its franchise operation. For example, signing a lease for a location that has not been properly evaluated and approved by the franchisor can have negative consequences. These can include poor sales which can result in significant operating losses. If a franchisor does not provide the franchisee the appropriate support regarding recruiting and hiring the right employees, it can negatively impact the franchise operation.

Site Selection Assistance

While a small unique type of franchises may use a homebased operation, most franchisees will need to find a location to operate their franchise. Site selection assistance is franchisor provided guidance that helps a franchisee identify and lease the most desirable franchise location. The right franchisee location can be critical to the success of many franchise concepts and for promoting the franchise brand. This is especially true for franchise concepts such as retail and food franchises, compared to a nonretail concept such as homecare or business services.

When a franchise operates from a poor location due to poor traffic flow, ingress or egress, its potential franchises revenues and earnings could be decreased. A poorly selected location often led to the closure of a franchise unit, either because of a franchisee's self- abandonment or the franchisor-initiated termination. Such closure could harm the franchise development program as future franchise prospects might equate a closed location to a poor franchise investment opportunity.

Site selection can include the services of a site selection firm, a demographic site selection software, or a national or local real estate company to find the most suitable available site for their franchisee. Some franchisors prefer to find and develop a site, which they will then lease to their franchisee. While most franchisees execute the site lease themselves, some franchisors have a different approach. When Christian Brothers Automotive, a franchise business that offers automotive repair and service products, looks for a site to present to the new franchisee for approval, it considers certain factors including customer demographics, access, traffic, competition, natural and man-made boundaries, and potential customer base. Once the site has been approved by a franchisee, Christian Brothers will purchase the site and construct the building to be leased to the franchisee.

When a franchise prospect has a location in mind before signing the franchise agreement, they must request prior approval from the franchisor before completing the transaction. This prevents both parties from making a major commitment before the franchise transaction is completed. Except for most home-based franchises, franchisors will retain the right to approve a location before the franchisee executes the lease. A typical franchisor site selection process is used by Ben's Barkek Place, in Roseville, California, which franchises retail health food pet stores that sell pet food, toys and related products. They provide site selection guidelines and other location advice and require their franchisees to find and select the site for a location within their territory, subject to franchisor approval.

As discussed in Chapter 5, the Franchise Operations Manual will include a chapter that provides guidance on franchise site selection and development. It should include important features of the site such as ease of access, available parking, traffic flow, existing businesses, and other features. There should be several alternative plans for building configurations, equipment, decor, and signage. Once the site is approved and before any construction or modifications are started, a copy of the blueprints and scope of work should be sent to the franchisor for approval. After approval, the franchisor should be available and prepared to help once work has started on the new location and be responsive to emails and telephone calls from the franchisee because site renovations could be delayed until questions are answered.

Franchisee Training

For franchisees to reproduce a successful business model in multiple locations, the franchisor is required to provide its franchisees the knowledge, skills, and ability to operate a franchise business.[4] Franchisee training is an important component of franchisor support. When franchisees are poorly trained, they may not be prepared to properly staff, open and operate their new franchise, potentially resulting in business unit failure, lengthy litigation, and severe damage to the franchise brand. Quality training is so essential, the training schedule, agenda, name, and title of presenters must be disclosed in the Franchise Disclosure Document under Item 11.

A survey of Millennials and younger workers by Accel in 2018 indicated that training is a major priority when that group is looking for employment. As this group represents the largest number of franchise employees, franchisors should formulate training as a top priority.[5] This strategy can enhance franchisee recruitment and improve employee performance.

Depending upon the complexity of the franchise operation and type of franchise business model, the training program can range from 1 to 6 weeks or longer. Training can take place at the franchisor's corporate office and can include onsite training at a company or franchise location. The training agenda should include presenters that are knowledgeable about a specific component of franchise operations, including marketing, product purchasing, and day-to-day franchise operations. It is beneficial to include franchisor staff who will interact with franchisees because they can bring their experience to the training program.

Some training programs are done in two segments: the first segment before a location is approved and prepared, and the second segment before the new franchise opening. This type of training schedule is frequently used in the franchise food sector. Kelly's franchise based in Saugus, Massachusetts, is a new casual fast-food franchise that has been operating independently since 1951. Its training program is comprehensive, consisting of 12 weeks of training for the franchise owner at Kelly's corporate headquarters and 8 weeks of training for management staff.

A well-structured training program must be designed so that a new franchisee is able to complete their training with enough knowledge to staff and prepare their new franchise for the opening. Follow-up training and support should continue as the franchisee is preparing to launch their new location. The timing of training is important, if training is done too far in advance of the new opening the participants might not retain all the information they were taught. Some franchisors provide training while the site is under construction while others train before the site is identified. From time to time, a franchisor may provide training to introduce new products, services, marketing programs, or franchise operating procedures. Given the benefits of technology, training can be provided in several ways from a virtual setting, webinar or at a conference or annual meeting. Despite their various setups and structures, these training programs often include the following assortment of topics:

i Business management topics aim to provide franchisees the basic knowledge and skills to manage their business units. It could cover leadership skills, motivation techniques, and other important management toolset.

ii Franchise operating procedures will provide franchisees both declarative and procedural knowledge on the operation of their franchise and the corresponding requirements. Franchisees need to understand and follow the proper procedures when operating their franchise, so the overall franchise system could maintain a consistent brand image and product quality for its franchise customers.

iii Human resource management is an important training segment that can ensure that franchisees will have a basic understanding of how to effectively obtain, allocate, and manage their human resources to effectively improve franchise performance. It provides guidelines on various employee-related issues, such as job descriptions for various position, the recruitment and selection of employees, and performance evaluation and management.

iv Franchise-specific marketing information will provide the franchisee with the product or service knowledge that will acquaint them with a keen understanding of the franchisee's customer offering. This can include, but would not be limited to, franchisees in the food business, residential and commercial services, home care, business services or retail products and fast food.

v Marketing aims to cover the foundation techniques and tools to help franchisees to communicate and engage their target customers to create and capture values. Some common topics include sample franchisor ads, product placement and layouts in the case of retail franchises, competition analysis, and pricing strategies.

vi Financial Management enable franchisees to better understand the allocation and management of financial resources relevant to the specific business activities of their franchise units. It includes the required financial reports for franchisors and often highlights the financial obligations of the franchisees, such as the amount and frequency of royalty and advertising fund payments. It often specifies bookkeeping software programs that a franchisee may be required to use.

Operational Services

In addition to franchisor support, franchisors frequently provide various operational services that enhance franchisees' ability to manage and operate their franchise unit. These operational services include payroll services, vendor purchase discounts, accounting, HR and IT support. Operational services are important as these could assist in franchise growth as it can allow franchisees to focus on their new franchise operation. These operational services can be an attractive feature that may appeal to prospective franchisees who are considering investing in the franchise.

The scope of these services can differ depending upon the type of franchise business, franchise operating system, and projected system growth. Franchisors that operate franchises that employ more than several people can provide payroll processing by contracting at lower fees with a payroll processing company such as ADP or Paychex. This enables a franchisee to process payroll, have withholdings made and produce payroll checks more efficiently and at less cost compared to doing it themselves. Franchisors in the food sector will specify required suppliers that provide franchisees quality products at reduced costs. Franchises in the commercial maintenance category such as ServePro a large residential and commercial franchisor will usually provide their franchisees with pre-packaged client service accounts that are pre-sold. This enables a franchisee to have ready business.

As a franchise system continues to grow, the franchisor can arrange for franchise purchase discounts from specific suppliers of required products, equipment, services, and supplies. For example, some franchisors might arrange for IT support, equipment, and accounting software to be purchased by franchisees from vendors at a discount. First Light Homecare, based in Cincinnati, Ohio, franchises homecare services. First Light provides its franchisees software for client scheduling services, accounting services and intranet access that supports their First Light homecare business. This enables their franchises to focus additional time on marketing their services and recruiting caregivers.

Franchisors may arrange for a third party to process payroll and perform mandatory withholdings and payments. SurePayroll, a division of Paychex, provides large and small franchises a Franchise Management Portal. Their portal enables franchises to easily process their payroll and will pay and file federal, state and local payroll taxes for the franchisee. SurePayroll cites their ability to free up valuable time for small franchise operations.

The Franchise Opening

A franchise opening consists of those activities that enable a franchisee to effectively introduce the new franchise unit to the media and public in the targeted franchise territory. The franchise opening is important as it represents the beginning of the franchisee's responsibility for managing their new franchise. It also serves as the beginning of the active franchisor–franchise relationship. The activities leading up to this point were preparatory in nature and did not require the franchisee to generate on-going revenues and expenses. Once the franchise is open and operating, the franchisee will expend capital until the franchise achieves break even and then profitability.

Executing a successful franchise opening can mean the difference between achieving franchisee financial goals or having the financial goals fall short. To a new franchisee preparing to startup, nothing can be more frustrating when they request assistance from their franchisor, and it's not provided in a timely fashion. As the first author who has participated in and attended numerous franchise openings, I have observed how a successful franchise opening could generate enthusiasm and instill confidence for both franchisees and franchisors. A successful franchise opening would translate to a positive customer experience because the franchisee and their employees will exhibit a positive and welcoming attitude, attracting more potential customers. For the franchisor, it could also result in a positive recommendation regarding the franchise program from the franchisee to subsequent franchise candidates.

Because of the importance of successful grand openings, savvy franchisors carefully design their grand opening program. They aim to create attention to the new franchise, generate consumer traffic, and provide a successful launch of the franchise. Creating attention to a new franchise opening can provide other benefits such as attracting potential employees and individuals who might be interested in a franchise opportunity in another market. While some franchisors will fund a portion of the grand opening, others may require the franchisee to expend a minimum amount on grand opening advertising and price promotions. The grand opening program usually consists of invitations to local business and political leaders, a ribbon cutting, and special product promotions.

The franchise opening offers franchisors and franchisee representatives an opportunity to meet special visitors and engage with the public. The franchisees, their employees, franchisor CEO, and franchisor staff should be in attendance and play active roles interacting with potential customers. While the franchisees are often an active member of the local community, local business and political leaders should be invited to help attract added attention to the event. The opening of a new franchise business is an opportunity for these stakeholders to be recognized and connected with franchisees and franchisors. It is also important to ensure that photographer and videographer are hired to record the grand opening for local media because they can help to generate publicity for the franchise. Except for smaller communities, onsite media coverage is usually reserved for franchises with strong branding such as a McDonald's or Chick-Fil-a or a franchise hotel chain. Each of which hire a significant number of employees which is newsworthy. Ribbon and Commemorative Scissors should be available for performing and recording the ribbon cutting ceremony.

During grand openings, one of the most effective ways to generate attention and consumer interest is through special product promotions. Various franchises offer different promotions. For example, product coupons can be provided to visitors to the grand opening who will be the first franchise customers. The coupons should offer substantial savings and be redeemable for a specific period. Some franchises offer 2–4 weeks of coupons. Certain businesses such as a home remodeling franchise that provide services or other types of service may hand out a certificate that provides a discount off services. Others, such as a franchise that provides residential home services like bathroom or kitchen remodeling could offer major discounts off the cost of a specific project while a homecare franchise may offer several hours of homecare services at a reduced cost for the first 30 days.

An example of an effective franchise grand opening program is how Chick-Fil-a promotes new franchise openings by featuring numerous specials and price promotions using direct mail and print media for several weeks. Some franchises distribute children's handouts for franchises have children as potential customers. This is especially appropriate for fast food franchisees that serve families. Franchisees also hand out key chains or other in-expensive gifts with the franchise logo and address.

Franchisors in the food and retail sector often use a "soft opening" for several weeks, prior to a grand opening. A "soft opening" enables a franchisor to train and provide support to the new franchisee and help fine-tune the franchise operation before conducting a full-blown grand opening program. This strategy can produce a trouble-free grand opening.

Grand opening services are usually large scale for highly recognized franchises, such as quick-service restaurant brands such as McDonald's and KFC. Their grand opening programs often include press releases and direct mail to potential customers that feature special price promotions. Conversely, franchises in the commercial, residential, and personal services category may have a modest onsite grand opening and unveil the grand opening with a campaign of direct mail, print, and electronic advertising.

After the franchise opening when the new franchise unit is up and running, franchisor staff should remain in contact with the franchisee for several weeks to ensure that the franchise is operating to their satisfaction and expectations. It is not unusual for some franchisees to be reluctant to contact their franchisor representative after the onsite grand-opening support has ended, the franchisor representative should take the initiative and contact the franchisee to ensure there are no unresolved problems. In fact, some franchisors provide post-grand opening assistance for several days or longer. The Huddle House based in Atlanta; Georgia has 400 locations that offer a Southern type of diner menu. It provides two to three weeks of pre-opening and post-opening assistance to its new franchisees. This type of onsite support is important because the franchisee will be operating their franchise for the first time. In some instances, a franchisor will assign a person to prepare the new owner for its grand opening and remain onsite during and after the grand opening.

Franchise Marketing

Another key component of franchisor support is the marketing and advertising assistance that franchisors can provide. Franchise marketing consists of the advertising, promotional, and marketing programs that enable franchisees to build strong relationships with their potential customers and generate consumer interest to purchase the franchisees products or services. Marketing is a key activity and integral component of the franchise business model because it can result in positive franchise branding enabling franchisees to increase their exposure, which in turn can lead to increased revenues. Marketing support is one of the main reasons why individuals invest in a franchise, because they can take advantage of the exposure, branding, and marketing support that a franchisor can provide.

Although certain franchisors may provide limited marketing support most agree to provide some marketing services. When franchisors fail to fulfill their marketing obligations and leave their franchisees responsible for promoting their own franchise units, it could impact franchisee performance. This can include dissatisfied franchisees and lower franchise sales. Also, franchisors that fail to provide adequate marketing support on behalf of their franchisees can suppress franchise brand awareness for the overall system. Next, we highlight important components of franchise marketing assistance that franchisors should focus on.

Implementing Marketing Programs

Franchise marketing program consists of both regional and national advertising activities intended to promote the franchise brand and increase consumer awareness in the local franchisee market. It often features major franchise products or services by utilizing effective advertising vehicles and has been considered as the most productive ways to promote franchise brand awareness.

Franchisors should follow three steps when launching its franchise marketing program. The first step is to provide marketing materials, consisting of advertising brochures and ad slicks for print advertising. Many franchisors provide these materials in a franchise start-up kit before the franchisee opens their new franchise. The second step is to identify those promotional items that will appeal to consumers in the target market to generate added revenues while preserving franchisee gross margin dollars. The last step is to measure the financial results of advertising programs to identify their effectiveness in generating additional revenues. As part of this process, it is important to solicit franchisee feedback to determine their satisfaction with franchise marketing program. As a franchise system grows, marketing activities will become more sophisticated and complex, prompting franchisors to include franchisees in a marketing committee to gain their insights and support for their advertising programs.

Franchisee Advertising Funding

Franchisors often administer an advertising fund that receives financial funds from its franchisees. This fund is in a segregated account separate from any royalty or other franchisee payments. The monies can be spent on local, regional, or national advertising activities. The use of advertising funds is important because they can be used on behalf of an entire franchise system or for targeted markets. Advertising funds enable franchisors to leverage advertising monies more efficiently than an individual franchisee. Once a certain amount of money in an advertising fund has been accumulated, franchisors usually establish an advertising committee, comprised of franchisor and franchisee representatives to effectively utilize advertising fund based upon a consensus of both parties.

The amount a franchisee contributes to an advertising fund is usually calculated as a percent of franchisee revenues ranging from 2% to 4% or in some cases a fixed dollar amount. For example, Property Stewards, a franchisor located just north of Atlanta, Georgia, manages and maintains vacation homes for clients, and has required its franchisees to contribute from 0% to 2% of monthly revenues to the national advertising fund.

Large franchise brands can have millions of dollars in their advertising fund, which allows them to aggressively promote its franchise locations and brand. For example, a national franchise brand could utilize its national advertising fund to pay for the high cost for a Super Bowl commercial. There have been several highly publicized lawsuits between franchisees and franchisors that involved the use of advertising funds. Burger King, KFC, Subway, and McDonald's are franchise brands that encountered major pushback from its franchisees regarding the application of advertising funds.

It's not unusual for a startup franchisor to defer contributions to the advertising fund until they have a minimum number of franchisees, such as five or more. Some startup franchisors would defer franchisee contributions to the advertising fund until there are a minimum number of locations, for example, 10 or more. The franchisor is obligated to keep the funds in a separate account and may be required to provide its franchisees an accounting of the fund upon request from franchisees or on an annual basis.

In addition to an advertising fund, franchisees are usually required to spend a minimum fixed dollar amount each month for advertising in their territory. This amount can range from $1,000 to $4,000 or more depending upon the type of franchise. Franchisees must document for the franchisor how much they spent on local advertising for each month and may be allowed to make a deficit spend in 1 month by exceeding the requirement in the following month.

Franchisor Pricing: Mandated versus Suggested Retail Prices

In terms of pricing, there are two main strategies that franchisors can employ regarding the price of products or services. One is mandated pricing, i.e., the practice of a franchisor requiring its franchisees to charge specific prices for products or services. Unlike employing this practice for company-owned locations, mandated pricing for franchisees can create major problems for franchisors because this practice may violate various federal and state statutes regarding allegations of price fixing, unfair competitive practices and legal challenges from franchisees that could end up in the courts.

The other strategy is the use of suggested retail pricing (SRP). SRP is the most prevalent approach in franchising and refers to a franchisor providing prices that a franchisee may charge but is not required to. Franchisors often specify these suggested prices in the franchise operations manual and in various franchisor communications. Franchisors must exercise caution regarding franchisee pricing. Although franchisor and franchisee marketing use promotional pricing in its advertising, franchisor pricing regimes should consist of SRPs rather than mandating prices for its franchisees. A common phase included in franchisor generated price promotion advertising is "At Participating Locations," which alleviates a franchisee from being required to participate in promotional pricing campaigns while providing notice to the customer. Despite some highly publicized disputes regarding certain franchisor promotional price advertising programs, involving Burger King, Subway, and KFC, most franchisees actively participate in franchisor price promotions without complaint.

Franchisor National Account Programs

A National Account (NA) program is a marketing strategy employed by franchisors to provide specific clients or customers beneficial pricing when purchasing franchise products or services from a franchisee or franchisor company location. An NA is important because it can provide franchisees with a pre-sold customer in their territory. Although there are price discounts granted to the NA, which can lower franchisee margins, an NA can be beneficial for the franchisor and its franchisees because it's a source of revenues that do not require extensive sales activities. The established business from an NA program can be an attractive feature of a franchise program and can be valuable when recruiting and signing new franchisees.

Thus, as the number of franchise locations grows, the franchisor may consider establishing a NA program. A franchisor will require a minimum number of locations to attract a potential NA customer. However, it is not necessary that the NA company be national in scope because it could have offices or business locations in a state or geographic region where there are franchisees. In most NA programs, the franchisor has the exclusive right to negotiate and enter into an agreement to provide products or services to a company and will have the option to provide its franchisees the right to service the National Account customer. If the National Account is in a franchisee territory, most franchisors will provide the franchisee the opportunity to service that account. However, if the franchisee declines or is not qualified, most franchisors will retain the right to delegate the business to another franchisee or can choose to service it themselves.

Examples of franchise services that could appeal to a potential NA customer may include maintenance, commercial, and sanitation services for property management firms, homecare franchises could establish a NA with health insurance providers and senior retirement communities and franchise fitness and gym memberships could be a perk provided by companies to their employees. JAN-PRO which is a large international commercial cleaning franchise based in Alpharetta, Georgia, has National Accounts throughout the United States with commercial building management companies. Its National Account Program features a National Account Manager, consolidated billing, financial reporting and franchisee access for service issues and requests. Franchisor CertaPro Painters provides painting services to multi-site Kindergarten, Tutoring, and Brick and Mortar Colleges and Universities accounts. As the first author, I worked for a franchisor that had NA customers that included McDonald's and Carrol Corporation the largest Burger King franchisee. These NAs added prestige to the franchisors brand and provided added revenue opportunities for our franchisees.

Government Contracts

Another important part of marketing programs is government contracts, i.e., agreements between Federal, state or local governments and non-government entities that allow the government to purchase products or services from a non-government entity. Government contracts are an important way for generating revenues and are frequently used by healthcare and medical staffing franchises. A number of personnel and temporary employee staffing franchises also use government contracting programs for their franchisees. Other government contracts are also available for a wide range of products and services that both local and federal government agencies may utilize.

Some franchisors choose to contract with local, state, or Federal government agencies that enables the franchisor and its franchisees to provide products or services to the contracting entity. To secure a government contract, a franchise or business must be a recognized business by the government which allows them to bid and compete for government contracts by submitting a business proposal for the execution of work, delivery dates, and other requirements.

The Small Business Administration provides a menu of services that provides guidance on bidding for government contracts. The SBA website states that it works with federal agencies to award twenty-three percent of prime government contract dollars to eligible small businesses. It also offers counseling and help to small business contractors and disadvantaged businesses may benefit from participating in the SBA 8(a) business development and mentor program for minority and disadvantaged small businesses that provides training and resources to help participating businesses compete in the federal contracting marketplace. National Account and government contracts can provide financial benefits for franchises, providing there are the available resources to apply for and administer the contracts.

An example of how franchisors utilize government contracts to attract franchisees is Pestmaster Services. It is a franchisor based in Bishop, California with franchises locations throughout the United States. It provides vegetation management, mosquito control, and traditional pest control services. Its franchisee recruitment advertising informs potential franchisees they could provide services under a government contract.

Franchisor Operations Support

Franchisor operations support and evaluations are the various activity's franchisor staff engages in to provide franchisees the ability to enhance or improve its franchise operation and financial performance. It includes processes that can support and improve franchisee operations, evaluate franchisee financial performance and assess franchisee compliance with franchise operating standards. These activities are important because as franchisor staff interact with franchisees, they will be able to learn how franchisees are performing, obtain information on competitors, and learn if a franchisee may require special assistance. Next, we describe three main components of franchise operation support: Franchise Site Visit, Franchisor Operations Representative, and Key Performance Indicators.

Franchise Site Visit

A franchisor site visit often involves a physical visit by a franchisor or representative to a franchisee operating location to gauge franchisee compliance. It is useful for obtaining market intelligence, feedback regarding competitors, marketing programs, and products. Its importance is illustrated by a recent survey, highlighting that 72% of franchisees did not think their field consultants spend enough time in the field visiting franchise units.[6] These site visits offer significant benefits for both parties. For example, the franchisor representative can provide the franchisee an assessment of their location appearance, product presentation, discuss current challenges the franchisee may be encountering and the competitive environment in the franchisee marketing area. The franchisee and franchisor can benefit from the personal interactions that provide each party what they expect from the site visits. It's also an opportunity to communicate with each other face-to-face which is more effective than emails or the telephone. Although site-visits are the most effective method of interaction, there are franchise brands, such as most homebased franchises, residential remodeling services, and business coaching franchises, that do not require site-visits.

The Franchisor Field Representative

Providing franchisor visits is the franchisor representative, also known as a regional director, field consultant or franchisee consultant. This position aims to support, advise, and audit the assigned franchisees. Franchisor Operations representatives play a significant role in franchise organizations as they are constantly monitoring and managing the performances of their assigned franchisees. Typically, a franchisor representatives may be assigned to 15 or more franchise locations, depending upon the type of franchise. Their responsibilities can include visiting franchise locations, inspecting the location for franchise system compliance, discussing franchise performance results with the franchisee and providing suggestions to improve the franchise operation.

The most important time for the first franchise site visit is during 1–2 months after opening or earlier. This is when the franchisee is enthusiastic about their new business coupled with high expectations and a willingness to work long hours to build a successful franchise. If the new franchise operation falters during this critical start-up phase, it could harm the franchisees confidence and jeopardize the future success of the franchise as a result. A franchisor that reviews and nurtures the performance of its new franchisees can contribute to a successful franchise network.

Franchisor field staff can visit their franchisees on a schedule that can range from every 2 weeks to once per month or quarterly. In less complex and home-based franchise systems not frequented by customers, such as residential remodeling and cleaning services a franchisor representative may visit the location once or twice per year or upon the request of the franchisee. As the first author, my regional directors were the most important resources I had. They provided me important franchise information and could be used to gather vital intelligence ranging from identifying the most successful franchise operations and signs of franchisee unrest to new competitor information.

The benefits from face-to-face contact are more effective compared to the use of email or a telephone conversation. Franchisor representatives need to keep in mind that a franchisee is not an employee of the franchisor and as such should be treated with a degree of respect in view of their contractual relationship with the franchisor and the franchisee's local knowledge of their marketplace. This means using a more consultative approach rather than a supervisory role used in company-owned operations. As a person invests in a franchise to capitalize on the knowledge and experience, the franchisor has acquired franchisees will expect that franchisor staff will interface with them and have competent staff to share franchisor knowledge.

From a franchisee perspective, a visit from a franchisor representative is usually welcomed because it enables the franchisee to provide feedback on their operation, learn about the performance of other franchisees and obtain advice and assistance if needed. It is important that a start-up franchisor makes more frequent contact and visits during the first year it is in operation. When a franchisee requests assistance from its franchisor regarding an operational or financial issue, it is important that the franchisor responds promptly to the request.

To help establish a business relationship, they can build a rapport with their franchisees and become familiar with individual franchisee and their operation. These tasks enable field representatives to develop in-depth knowledge on why some franchisees are more successful than others. These findings should be documented with any recommendations provided to the franchisees and franchisors. This should include, where necessary, a plan of action that the franchise should implement. Some franchisees use a checklist or other form for documenting the results of the site visit.

As indicated at the beginning of this chapter, one of the leading causes of franchisee dissatisfaction is a lack of franchisor support. Because this can sometimes lead to disputes and litigation between the parties, the importance of proper franchisor documentation in the relationship between a franchisor and its franchisees cannot be over emphasized. Proper franchisor documentation can motivate a franchisee to take corrective action and may discourage a franchisee from escalating an issue into litigation. Finally, the availability of accurate and available documentation can result in exonerating franchisors unfairly accused of failing to support a franchisee.

It can be challenging for a franchisor representative to address a franchisee's operating and performance deficiencies because franchisees will have more knowledge about their individual franchise business than the representative assigned to support them. To accomplish these, we next discuss how franchisors should use KPIs to acquire key operating data to track and improve franchisee performance.

Key Performance Indicators

Managing franchise financial performance is a process that includes the gathering of individual franchise financial data, analyzing the data, and identifying the performance results to determine how each franchisee and the overall franchise system is performing. It is an important process for building a successful franchise program. When a franchisor acquires key franchisee financial data, it can be used to ascertain the operational and financial performance of individual franchisees and the overall franchise system. This information enables franchisors to compare franchisee and franchise system performance and identify any deviations.

To manage franchisee financial performance, franchisors often utilize KPIs to capture specific financial data submitted by each franchise. The corresponding monthly report is an effective method to measure franchisee operational and financial performance. This process can serve as an early warning system to identify franchises that are under performing. KPIs help to maintain operating standards and identify franchisees who are not meeting important goals.[7]

Following are KPIs that franchises use:

i   Gross Sales is one of the fundamental measures of franchisee performance. It is also used to calculate franchisee royalty payments and other fees like advertising fund payments. Franchisors often use gross sales to rank franchisee performance. This indicator provides information on how much sales a franchise location is generating which would allow for comparisons among franchise locations.
ii Monthly sales growth by percent enables the franchisor to identify and compare the rate of sales growth or decline among franchisees and a way to rank franchisee sales growth into quartiles. This information can be used to diagnose why some franchisees perform better than others.
iii Franchisee monthly gross margin percent and dollars are metrics that indicates the gross margins that each franchisee is achieving. As gross margin dollars pay the expenses, this data can be used to analyze why some franchisees have higher gross margin dollars than others. In some cases, it could be type of products or services that a franchise customers purchase.
iv Franchisee profitability is an important KPI used to identify which franchisees are profitable and those who may be losing money. Like other KPIs, these data can be ranked, and certain franchise operations diagnosed to identify why some franchisees are more profitable than others.

The usage of KPIs can vary depending upon the type of franchise. For example, a report by Franconnect illustrates that certain KPIs that are mainly useful for franchise food concepts. For example, Speed of Service which is (Food Order Time) minus (Food Delivery Time) is a good metric for time-starved customers and does not require any new data points. A Point-of-Sale register used to record customer purchases can be used to automatically measure the time the customer walks in or drives up to a restaurant to the time when the food is delivered to them based on your kitchen display system.[8]

Using KPIs is an efficient way to evaluate and compare franchisee financial performance. This is easier and timelier than extracting this information from franchisee quarterly financial statements. Franchisors should implement the required technology to pull KPI franchise data from their franchisees to provide franchise decision-makers the information they need more quickly.[9]

Summary

Franchisor support is one of the most important services that franchisees expect to receive from their franchisor. Individuals invest in a franchise to benefit from the expertise and knowledge that can be transferred from the successful franchise business model. Because of such expectation, a lack of franchisor support can adversely impact the franchise-franchisor relationship and franchisee performance. Franchisors should be diligent when supporting its franchisees and comply with its contractual obligations. Ultimately, franchisors need to ensure its franchisees can enhance their ability to operate their business more effectively via providing supports in the training, operation, and marketing areas. It can also include additional franchisor services, such as vendor purchase discounts, human resources support, financial, and technical services. These support and services are required to be provided in the Franchise Agreement and Franchise Operations Manual.

It is important that franchisee operations are audited on a periodic basis to confirm they are complying with their contractual franchise operational and financial obligations. Franchisors can also measure the operational and financial performance of their franchisees using KPIs. Based on these indicators, they can then counsel and advise those franchisees that may require operational assistance and counseling. Ultimately, the franchisor needs to carefully manage these support and services areas to ensure the development and growth of a successful franchise company.

Notes

1 Blut, M., Backhaus, C., Heussler, T., Woisetschläger, D., Evanschitzky, H., & Ahlert, D. (2011). What to expect after the honeymoon: Testing a lifecycle theory of franchise relationships. *Journal of Retailing, 87,* 306–319.

2 Frazer, L., & Winzar, H. (2005). Exits and expectations: Why disappointed franchisees leave. *Journal of Business Research, 58*, 1534–1542.

3 Franconnect Blog (2021). *How to do On-going Franchisor Monitoring Right.* https://blog.franconnect.com/how-to-do-ongoing-franchisee-monitoring-right

4 LaVan, H., Coye, R. W., & Latona, J. C. (1986). Training and development in the franchisor – Franchisee relationship. *Journal of European Industrial Training, 12*(3), 27–31.

5 Hackel, E. (2019). The value of ongoing training for building franchise success. Franchising.com

6 Franconnect (2021). High-impact franchisee engagement. https://blog.franconnect.com/franconnect-franchise-library-2020/high-impact-franchisee-engagement

7 McCoy, R. (2018). *Franchising KPIs and Their Use in Crisis Avoidance.* LIGS University.

8 Franconnect Blog (2021). *The 15 Most Important restaurant KPIs* August, 2021 *The 15 Most Important restaurant KPIs.* https://blog.franconnect.com/the-15-most-important-restaurant-franchise-kpis?utm_campaign=FranConnect%20Blog&utm_medium=email&_hsmi=150901962&_hsenc=p2ANqtz-9zpgvYLWlL8Cew-X5MMJfLuwaKCPwS1HqlUjminbmTRKYD4rpRbTThdEmcwk8wGMItROP6-qXmYCpX1dwh1S_aOIAm6aQ2n0NDtm61yNPKm443Zd4&utm_content=150901962&utm_source=hs_email

9 Franconnect (2021). High-impact franchisee. *Engagement.* https://blog.franconnect.com/how-to-do-ongoing-franchisee-monitoring-right

Chapter 9

Franchise Relationship Management

In Chapter 8, we discussed the importance of administering and supporting franchisees. We then elaborated on the essential franchisor support services, including franchisee training, onsite franchise site visits, providing marketing and advertising programs, human resource, payroll programs, and favorable vendor purchase programs. Franchisees have an expectation to receive support from their franchisor along with properly managed services to ensure the development and growth of a successful franchise company. The franchisee–franchisor relationship needs to be carefully managed to ensure a harmonious productive relationship. Successful franchise performance results ensue from dependable franchisor support and Franchise Relationship Management (FRM).

FRM is a franchisor strategy that utilizes procedures, policies, and tactics to promote a positive relationship between a franchisor and its franchisees. It is one of several important activities, including franchise development and support, that franchisors should focus on after the emerging franchisor has introduced new franchisees into its network. The importance of positive franchise relations cannot be overstated because it's a characteristic of successful franchise operations.

In this chapter, we begin with a description of the various phases a franchisee passes through during their relationship with the franchisor. We then present the FRM strategy including specific tactics that can produce positive outcomes between a franchisor and franchisees. These tactics include managing conflict between the franchisor and its franchisees, surveying and measuring franchisee satisfaction levels, evaluating and monitoring franchisee financial performance, as well as how to utilize franchisee associations to maintain open lines of communication between franchisees with their franchisor. We conclude with how FRM can help to avoid and manage litigation between a franchisor and its franchisees by using alternative dispute resolution.

DOI: 10.4324/9781003034285-9

The Phases of a Franchisee

Based upon our experience, we have found that a franchisee passes through certain phases from the beginning to the end of their franchise ownership. It's important for franchisors to be aware of these phases and how they can impact franchisor–franchisee relations.

The initial franchisee phase starts during franchisee–franchisor interactions before the franchisee signs the franchise agreement and continues through the franchising process. During this phase, the franchisor usually establishes expectations on the part of the franchisee. For example, if the franchisor representative states that franchisor staff responds promptly to a franchisee's request for assistance the franchisee will expect to receive this benefit when they begin operating the franchise. During this phase franchise candidates usually ask questions that deal with the subject of franchisor support. For example, how often would a franchisor representative visit the franchisee location, and how does the franchisor assistance process work? If the franchisor representative misinforms the franchisee and the franchisor fails to deliver when the person is a franchisee it can result in a negative impression that can detract from a positive relationship.

Once a franchisee opens their new franchise, and assuming that they have received the proper training and initial support, the franchisee will be enthusiastic about their new franchise. This can help to establish a harmonious relationship with the franchisor. During this operational phase, most franchisees settle into a performance level that is either acceptable or unacceptable to them and their franchisor. This is a critical phase in FRM because franchisees that fail to exhibit current or potential success need to be identified and franchisors need to provide assistance. Otherwise, this is when underperforming franchisees start to doubt the viability of their franchise operation and are trapped on a trajectory leading to failure, resulting in serious conflicts with their franchisor.[1]

Most franchisees eventually enter a final phase of their relationship with their franchisor when they decide to sell their franchise. If there has been a positive relationship with the franchisor during their tenure as a franchisee, it can result in a positive end to the relationship. This can assist the franchisee in obtaining a favorable selling price for their franchise rights and may validate the quality of the franchise brand to potential franchisees. It is important that franchisors are aware of how the franchisor–franchisee relationship evolves so its staff is prepared to respond to franchisee issues and challenges as a franchisee passes through various phases as a franchisee.

Conflict Management between Franchisees and Franchisors

Conflict management represents practices and tactics that franchisors implement to resolve disagreements between the franchisor and its franchisees. Disagreements in a franchise relationship can occur anytime from the franchise grand opening when they decide to sell their franchise. When conflicts are unresolved, it can lead to major disputes, litigation and can carry over into negative feedback to other franchisees and franchise candidates. Franchisors should employ conflict management to prevent disagreements with their franchisees from escalating into a major dispute or legal actions.

The Source of Franchisee Franchisor Conflicts

Franchise conflicts can arise when the franchisee or franchisor has a disagreement with the other party or fails to fulfill their contractual obligations. Sources of conflict can result from specific actions by a franchisee or franchisor. If a franchisor fails to fulfill a commitment to a new franchisee that was made before the franchise transaction was consummated, the franchisee will be disappointed and may seek redress from the franchisor. For example, the franchisee reports a problem and requests assistance, and fails to receive a response from the franchisor. In this case, franchisor management should contact the franchisee and advise them they will review and determine why the franchisee failed to receive a response from the franchisor.

Another cause of conflict is when a franchisee fails to comply with their obligations to comply with certain franchise operating standards. For example, a franchisee does not spend the required amount of money on advertising, opens their location late, or closes earlier than the required hours of operations. In these cases, a franchisees' continued failure to comply could result in a serious conflict. The best way to resolve this conflict is to verbally remind the franchisee of their contractual obligations and document in writing. In addition, the franchisor representative should explain to the franchisee why it's important to comply with their obligations using the example of how they would react if a neighboring franchisee did the same thing which could harm the franchise brand.

A different source of conflict can occur when a franchisor sells competing products through alternative retail channels in a franchisees' territories. For instance, a franchisor grants supermarkets the right to sell the same franchise products in an existing franchisee's territory, although the franchise agreement may grant the franchisor this right. This type of conflict can be minimized or avoided by sharing some of the financial benefits from the supermarket product sales, which is exactly what franchisor Dunkin' Donuts did in the case of its coffee pod sales.

Tools for Managing Conflict in the Franchise Relationship

Avoiding conflicts between a franchisor and its franchisees can be achieved by employing franchisor practices that prevent conflicts from escalating. Good communication, measuring franchisee performance, and identifying franchisee satisfaction levels are the most important factors in successful FRM regardless of franchise system size whether emerging or mature.

Effective Franchise Communication

This is a process whereby; franchisees should expect they can bring their questions and concerns to their franchisor and receive a timely and adequate response. Some franchisors have a policy that states, except for an emergency requiring a rapid response, a franchisee should receive a response to an important question or concern within 24 hours. Franchisors have an obligation to inform their franchisees about important changes to franchise operating model, upcoming marketing programs, and other events that can affect franchisee operations. Failing to inform its franchisees about these changes in a timely manner can lead to franchisee dissatisfaction.

Communication remains a critical feedback mechanism regarding franchise performance and the direction of future relationships.[2] This is a tool that should be used while a new franchisee is in the early phase of their franchise operation. As the first author, I reported to a CEO who learned of a franchisor representative failing to respond to a franchisee issue which led to a disgruntled franchisee. The CEO asked me if they should call the franchisee and if so would it help calm the situation and appease the franchisee. This gesture by the CEO indicates how important communication can be to maintain and promote positive franchise relations.

Another way a franchisor can prevent conflicts from escalating is by a franchisor soliciting feedback from its franchisees using its field representatives, franchise meetings, and conference calls. When a franchisor is out of touch and unaware of the concerns of its franchisees these concerns can escalate into major disputes. For emerging franchisors, the CEO should personally contact select franchisees on a regular basis to obtain feedback regarding their performance and whether they have any concerns regarding the franchisor support. This is an important tool for a new franchisor because most new franchisees require nurturing and welcome hearing from the CEO.

An example of how important good communication is to the franchise relationship is offered by Jimmer Bennett a franchisee with Unishippers who states that the key to his strong relationship with his franchisor starts with honest and trustworthy communication, not just the occasional email check in, or holiday text message. Being in the logistics and transportation industry, Bennett states that events can happen over the course of a day, when he needs to rely on the franchisor for assistance.

Measuring Franchisee Performance

As discussed in Chapter 8, franchisors measure franchisee financial performance by acquiring monthly franchisee reports on key performance indicators (KPIs). A KPI is a measurement of a specific set of metrics that indicates how a franchise is performing against its goals and the performance of individual and collective franchisees in the same franchise system.

KPIs are identified by collecting and tabulating specific franchise financial information. KPIs should include monthly sales, gross margin percent and dollars, payroll costs, and other pertinent franchise financial data. A franchisor should guide each franchisee toward achieving their financial goals, therefore it is essential that the franchisor is aware of whether their franchisees are meeting their financial objectives by identifying and comparing their individual financial performance.

KPI is a tool that franchisors should use as part of their operational and FRM strategy. Identifying how each franchisee is performing enables the franchisor to identify which franchisees are performing well and the reasons why. They also need to identify those franchisees who are performing below the top performers and learn why. A potential source of poor franchise relations is when certain franchisees are either unprofitable or dissatisfied with their financial results. By monitoring franchisee performance, a franchisor can provide operational guidance and if necessary, grant financial assistance such as deferring royalty fee payments for a period of time. These interventions that assist deserving franchisees are important for enhancing positive franchise relations because they demonstrate the commitment by the franchisor to individual franchisee success.

Measure Franchisee Satisfaction Levels

Franchisee satisfaction levels are measured when a franchisor surveys its franchisees and tabulates the results to identify how satisfied franchisees are with various franchisor support, services, and the total franchise program. Identifying franchisee satisfaction levels are important during the various phases of a franchisee operation, especially during the initial 1–3 years which is when franchisees are at a critical phase of their franchise operation. Measuring franchisee satisfaction levels enables a franchisor to identify and address those areas that require improvement and the opportunity to identify and correct any major problem areas their franchisees may have.

Surveys should be conducted by the franchisor or a third party that specializes in measuring franchisee satisfaction levels. The process consists of franchisees being requested to respond to various questions using a rating system. For example, 1 to 5, with 5 being "totally agree" and 1 "being totally disagree." Survey questions should be designed to conform to the franchise category and include franchisor support, franchisee profitability, franchisor response, and the effectiveness of franchisor marketing programs.

After a franchise system has several franchisees, the franchisor should begin to survey its franchisees to measure satisfaction levels. For emerging franchise systems with less than 10–15 franchisees, satisfaction surveys can be done by telephone or even in face-to-face meetings. As a franchise system gets larger some franchisors use a third party to conduct their franchise satisfaction surveys. These companies are specialized in conducting satisfaction surveys. One company is Franchise Business Review (FBR), located in Portsmouth, New Hampshire. According to its CEO, Eric Stites, a common complaint found in FBR's research is that franchisees often feel uninvolved with their franchisor when key decisions are dictated by the franchisor. Franchise companies with high satisfaction scores have learned to engage and involve their franchisees using clear, transparent, two-way communication. Sites believe that the top franchisors allow their franchisees to provide feedback which fosters a collaborative, win–win culture. Sites also stated that better-performing franchise brands manage to keep their marketing and technology-driven programs less complicated which demonstrates to their franchisees the effectiveness and return on investment these tools can provide.

Whether franchisors conduct their own satisfaction survey or use a third party, it is important to identify how franchisees rate critical components of their franchise system and their satisfaction with the franchise program. Obtaining regular franchisee feedback is a necessary requirement for maintaining positive franchise relations. Knowing how satisfied or dissatisfied franchisees are regarding various aspects of their franchise performance can enable a franchisor to address those issues that can negatively impact FRM.

Additional FRM Tools

In addition to managing and avoiding conflicts with their franchisees, practicing good communication techniques, and measuring franchisee satisfaction levels franchisors can employ other tools that can enhance FRM. When combined these components will provide the proper business climate where the franchisor and its franchisees can achieve and maintain a continuing positive relationship.

a   Documented Franchisor Operating Principles: Franchisors should have an organized set of principles or practices they follow. Documented franchisor operating principles and practices are published guidelines that franchisor staff follow in the administration and support of their franchisees. It's important that franchisors have their principles fully documented in their franchise operations manual or website so that their employees, existing and prospective franchisees are fully aware of franchisor business and operating standards.

An example of franchisor operating principles is shared by Mark Jameson, Executive VP of Propelled Brands a franchisor based in Carrolton, Texas. The four principles that guide Propelled Brands are to:

1   Drive franchisee profitability
2   Promote and drive top-line franchisee growth
3   Grow the franchise system
4   Assure that franchisee satisfaction is measured

In addition, Propelled brands use a third party to survey franchisees and conduct a confidential company survey that is shared with the franchisor employees. They have a Franchise Advisory Council and every six weeks the CEO has a virtual town hall meeting that all franchisees can attend. There is a National Advertising board that includes six elected franchisees. A Diversity and Inclusion Task Force was formed by the franchisor in 2020 to help attract potential franchisees.

b   Franchisor FRM Leadership: Regardless of the role franchisor staff may occupy it's important for each employee to be aware of the importance of positive franchise relations. Franchisor leadership in FRM occurs when all members of the organization act in a professional manner and are responsive to the needs of franchisees. Important franchisee issues or problems should be brought to the attention of franchisor leadership to devise an appropriate course of action if needed. As the first author, I've been responsible for conducting meetings with franchisor support staff to communicate the importance of good FRM practices.

c   A Franchise committee: A franchise committee is a representative group of franchisees who meet with select franchisor staff on a periodic basis. The most frequently used committee is a franchise marketing or advertising committee. This is an effective vehicle for supporting FRM because it enables franchisees to provide input regarding proposed franchisor marketing and advertising initiatives. An emerging franchisor with a minimum of 25 franchisees should establish an advertising or marketing committee that includes franchisor and franchisee representatives. It can provide a forum for the franchisor to obtain feedback from their franchisees especially when the franchisor is considering implementing operational or marketing changes that can have a significant impact on franchisee operations.[3]

d   Franchisors Share Best Practices: Franchisee best practices are operating practices that a franchisee employs to enhance their performance. Best practices can include employee recruitment and hiring tips, unique marketing practices, product enhancements, and other methods that are transferable and which can improve franchisee revenues and profitability. Franchisor field representatives are usually aware of certain franchisee best practices because they communicate with their franchisees on a regular basis and discuss their operating practices.

It's important that franchisors share successful franchisee best practices because it can improve franchise relations. Soliciting and sharing franchisee best practices can lead to new processes and programs that can enhance franchise operations. An effective method for sharing best practices is for the franchisor to solicit examples from franchisees and share this information in a bulletin or newsletter. This will ensure other franchisees are aware of best practices and support positive FRM. Sharing what successful franchisees do can encourage other franchisees to do the same.[4] For example, McDonald's Filet of Fish and Big Mac sandwich were both the creation of franchisees.

Franchisee Owners Associations and Franchise Advisory Councils

One of the most effective ways to improve franchise relations is via a franchisee owners association (FOA) or franchise advisory council (FAC). An FOA is operated and funded by franchisee representatives. The FOA will include by-laws governing the election of association officers, payment of dues, and functional procedures. An FOA is an independent organization comprised of franchisees and administered by a consultant or individual experienced in franchising or organizational leadership. Another franchisee organization is an FAC, which is a joint association or affiliation typically comprised of fifty percent franchisor and franchisee representatives. An FAC meets several times per year and is encouraged to share any significant franchisee issues with the franchisor and will discuss and establish potential operational and marketing initiatives. In most cases, the franchisor will pay for the travel, lodging, and cost of meals for the FAC meetings.

Keith R. Miller, a Subway franchisee of 32 years and franchisee advocate testified before the United States Senate Economic Policy Subcommittee on franchising. He stated in part, that the keys to positive franchise relations are achieved when franchisees are represented and can provide feedback to the franchisor.

If franchisees believe that the FAC fails to meet their needs, is not independent or effective in negotiating disputes with the franchisor, the franchisees may convert the FAC to a new independent franchisee association. For example, in the Denny's franchise system, the franchisor had established an advisory council to address the concerns of franchisees and to give the franchise community the ability to communicate with Denny's corporate. In November 1997, however, the DFAC was replaced by the independent, franchisee-sponsored Denny's Franchisee Association to eliminate the franchisor's veto power over the association's decisions and to allow the franchisees to develop bargaining power with outside vendors.[5]

There are several benefits of franchisee organizations. First, franchisees may perceive the franchisor to be more willing to engage in fair dealing with franchisees, as they have an opportunity to express their lack of satisfaction with certain aspects of the franchise. This will help contribute to enhanced franchise relations. Second, franchisees who are members of a franchisee association may have a greater sense of loyalty and commitment to the franchise because the franchisor has displayed its respect for the franchisees by recognizing them as an organization. An FOA or FAC can be used as a sounding board whereby the franchisor can introduce proposed products or strategies to obtain feedback from the franchisee representatives.

By soliciting feedback and suggestions from their franchisees the franchisor is demonstrating a commitment to the franchise network as opposed to the franchisor mandating a change. Both parties can speak openly at meetings and address sensitive topics in a productive way. This can help to promote a relationship with added trust among the franchisor and franchisee representatives. For example, Mosquito Joe, a mosquito control franchise based in Virginia Beach, Virginia encourages and advocates open communication with its franchisees. When a franchise system reaches a certain size it's not unusual for the franchisees to transition from a FAC to an independent franchisee association. This is common with large franchise systems like Subway, Wendy's, Burger King, and McDonald's, which also has a McDonalds Black Owners Association.

Edwin Shanahan has been the Executive Director at DDIFO, Inc. (Dunkin Donuts Independent Franchise Owners Association) for 9 years. Mr. Shanahan states that there are important differences between an FAC, which involves the participation of the franchisor and an Independent Franchisee Association, which is operated solely by franchisees. He states that with an FAC and its close relationship with the franchisor because it is paying for dinners, lodging, and other expenses, some franchisees may be reluctant to provide feedback regarding important concerns of other franchisees they represent. He, states this is a natural inclination for franchisees who receive certain benefits from the franchisor. In comparison, an FOA is a separate organization operated and funded by franchisees for franchisees. Shanahan states it is in the best interest of franchisors to want honest feedback from its franchisees and credible input regarding important issues or complaints.

As the first author, I have established, organized, and administered several FACs as the franchisor representative. We would arrange for bi-annual meetings in various off-site locations and pay for all the expenses. Although our use of a FAC could possibly inhibit some franchisees from being candid in terms of reporting franchisee concerns, that wasn't my experience. Whichever type of group a franchisor decides to advocate, it is important that the franchisor obtains the advice and guidance of their franchise attorney regarding the type of organization and its guidelines. Whether using a FAC or dealing with an independent franchisee association, franchisors shouldn't fear the formation of a franchisee organization. If they do, they may face far greater problems in the future.

Avoiding and Managing Franchise Litigation

As we indicated, conflicts and disagreements can arise between a franchisor and franchisee from time to time due to the contractual relationship between the franchisor and its franchisees on occasion, a disagreement can be so serious that it could escalate into a lawsuit. Commonly referred to as litigation it's a complaint by one party, the plaintiff against another party, the defendant that is brought in a court of law. The franchisor or franchisee can be the plaintiff or defendant based upon who initiates the litigation. All litigation, arbitration, and related settlements are required to be disclosed in Item 3 of the Franchise Disclosure Document. Unless a franchisor has no choice it's important that franchisors take steps to avoid litigation because it can be financially costly, must be disclosed in the FDD, and can negatively affect franchise relations.

An example of a dispute leading to litigation is when a franchisor continually prices advertised products or services that result in a reduction of franchisee gross margin dollars. This causes franchisees to question this practice which leads to a confrontation requesting the franchisor to stop or reduce it. A lawsuit brought by Subway, MacDonald's, and Burger King franchisee associations over the past number of years, although ultimately settled, impacted the reputation of both franchise brands. Had the franchisors attempted to amicably resolve these disputes at the beginning it may have avoided litigation, saved expenses, and avoided harm to franchise relations. Each of these franchisors had powerful independent franchisee associations which can be formidable opponents of franchisor decisions.

In some cases, litigation is unavoidable, for example when a franchisee commits an egregious act and fails to cease and desist. For example, a home care franchisee continues to fail to properly qualify caregiver credentials, which could place their clients at risk and damage the reputation of the franchise brand.

Its important franchisors try to avoid litigation because of the legal costs, poor publicity, and potential negative impact on the franchisor's reputation. In addition, when a prospective franchisee and their franchise attorney review Item 3 in the FDD any franchise litigation is sure to be scrutinized. An unusual amount of litigation in relation to the size of the franchise system can end any interest by a prospective franchisee. A strategy franchisors often employ is to have a financial resolution by agreeing to purchase the franchise back. This will avoid litigation and its disclosure in the FDD and end a disagreeable relationship between the parties.

A major cause of franchise litigation is when a franchisor engages in aggressive and deceptive franchises practices which can harm prospective and existing franchisees. For example, Quiznos which franchised sandwich shops and had experienced dynamic growth in the early 2000s was levied one of the largest financial penalties in franchise history in 2010. The settlement was the result of four separate lawsuits. One lawsuit included a memorandum by a Quiznos lawyer in 2003 that stated that 40% of Quiznos units weren't breaking even. Between 2007 and 2017, Quiznos shrunk from 4,700 U.S. locations to fewer than 400. John Gordon, principal of Pacific Management Consulting Group, stated that Quiznos' franchise strategy, its store-level economics and business model were deeply flawed.[6]

Preventing Disputes from Escalating into Franchise Litigation

It is important that franchisors seek to manage and control serious disputes between them and their franchisees. Seeking a resolution that can satisfy both parties should be the primary objective. If there is a potential threat to the franchise brand, caused by the franchisee that remains unresolved, the franchisor may have no option except to take legal action. In many cases, resolving a dispute and avoiding litigation between a franchisor and franchisee can be achieved with the assistance of the FAC, the Franchisee Association or intervention by a well-respected franchisee. One of these parties may have sufficient influence and experience to help broker a resolution and avoid a lawsuit.

Certain franchisor practices, like properly documenting the support and assistance it provides its franchisees can discourage a dissatisfied franchisee and their attorney from filing a lawsuit. By demonstrating the totality of assistance, the franchisor has provided a franchisee can be useful in the event a franchisee chooses to file a lawsuit. As the first author, I've had the experience of being involved in numerous franchisee lawsuits against the franchisor. In those cases where we prevailed, it was the result of having a carefully documented franchisee file. When the outcome was unfavorable it was the result of sloppy or poor documentation by a member of franchisor staff. I was also in both Federal and state court and participated in Arbitration proceedings. It's by experience that arbitration is a more effective process for the adjudication of major franchisor–franchisee disputes.

Alternative Dispute Resolution

A common business and legal practice to resolve disputes and prevent litigation is to utilize Alternative Dispute Resolution (ADR) which is included in almost every franchise agreement. ADR consists of methods to avoid or settle litigation by engaging the franchisor and franchisee in a structured process that can resolve a dispute. ADR is less costly and disruptive to both parties and avoids the consequences of participating in a courtroom engaged in a formal legal process. There are two forms of ADR, Arbitration and Mediation, which can be used to resolve serious disputes and prevent litigation:

Arbitration

Arbitration is a procedure in which a dispute between two parties, for example, a franchisor and a franchisee are submitted, by the agreement of the parties, to one or more arbitrators who make a binding decision on their dispute. By engaging in arbitration, the parties avoid court litigation. Franchise agreements typically include arbitration as the required method of dispute resolution in lieu of formal litigation in a courtroom.

Mediation

Mediation involves the use of a neutral, third-party Mediator that like Arbitration can be agreed upon by the parties. The Mediator meets with the parties and their lawyers, serving as a facilitator for discussion and negotiation that can resolve the dispute. When using a Mediator, no decision or ruling is imposed on either the franchisor or franchisee, and neither party is required to accept a specific outcome or proposed

Table 9.1 Major Differences between Litigation, Arbitration, and Mediation

Litigation	Arbitration	Mediation
More costly than ADR	Less costly than litigation	Least costly
Public	Private	Private
Formal process. Set rules	Less formal than litigation	Least formal
Inflexible rigid process	Simplified rules of evidence and procedure	Very flexible
Judge is appointed	Parties can choose substantive expert(s) to serve as arbitrator(s)	Parties can select an arbitrator
More complex with depositions	May not require depositions	N/A
Easily appealed	Difficult to appeal	N/A
Decision can take time	Decision provided faster	Parties agree to result
	Process can be designed by the participants	Mediator may be poorly qualified

resolution. A Mediator seeks to help the parties reach their own mutually acceptable solution (Table 9.1).

The Franchise Mediation Program

In 1994 a Franchise Mediation Program, was formed in collaboration with the International Institute for Conflict Prevention and Resolution which is a non-profit alliance of corporations and law firms founded in 1979 to develop alternatives to the high costs of litigation. This program has been endorsed by the International Franchise Association, Asian American Hotel Owners Association, and the American Association of Franchisees and Dealers, and has been used by franchisors, franchisees, and franchisee associations. The Conflict Prevention and Resolution procedure is initiated by a Dispute Letter, sent by either the franchisor or the franchisee to the other party and the Conflict Prevention and Resolution. If accepted by the recipient, the Conflict Prevention and Resolution Procedure requires the parties to attempt to resolve their differences through negotiations.

Franchise Relationship Management is a critical component of franchisor operations. Positive franchise relations can enable a successful franchise program to prosper, while poor franchise relations can sap franchisee morale and stifle enthusiasm among franchisees. When there is a lack of trust between a franchisor and its franchisees it will become difficult for prospective franchisees to obtain a positive validation of the franchise program from existing franchisees. If a prospective franchisee contacts an existing franchisee to obtain feedback on franchisor support and assistance, a poor relationship between the franchisee and its franchisor can elicit negative responses. When the state of franchise relations is positive, there is a sense of balance within the franchise system. Both parties are achieving their objectives and working in a supportive manner to grow the franchise brand.

Summary

We discussed FRM which is a strategy that should be implemented by all franchisors regardless of size. An FRM strategy should be based on supporting franchisees and managing conflicts between a franchisor and their franchisees. We presented how an effective way to establish positive franchise relations is by the franchisor enabling effective and timely communication with their franchisees and measuring franchisee performance using KPIs. We discussed how measuring franchisee satisfaction levels have been demonstrated to be an effective way to identify which franchisees are achieving satisfactory financial results and those that may require assistance. Also, we stated that franchisors can promote positive franchise relations by empowering franchisees to provide feedback to the franchisor through a FAC or Independent Franchisee Association which enables franchisee representatives to participate with their franchisor in important decision-making. A marketing or advertising committee that includes franchisee representatives can also boost the level of positive franchise relations. Finally, we discussed how disputes can arise between a franchisor and its franchisees and why there should be a process to avoid disputes from escalating into litigation. A dispute resolution process can be used to lead to a fair outcome for both parties and help to avoid costly litigation between the franchisor and its franchisees.

Notes

1 Wincent, W. S. (2019). The basics of franchising. The relationship. *International Franchise Association Newsletter*. https://www.franchise.org/franchise-information/the-basics-of-franchising-the-relationship
2 William, R., Meek, B. D., Sramek, M. S., Baucus, R., & Germain, R. (2011). Commitment in franchising: The role of collaborative communication and a franchisee's propensity to leave. *Entrepreneurship Theory and Practice, 35*(3), 559–581.
3 Badrinarayanan, V., Kyung-Min, K., & Taewon, S. (2016). Brand resonance in franchising relationships: A franchisee-based perspective. *Journal of Business Research, 69*(10), 3943–3950. McCoy College of Business Administration, Texas State University, Silla University, South Korea.
4 Higginson, D. (2019). Building a culture of information sharing improves operations, boosts franchise relations, and saves time. *International Franchise Association Bulletin*.

5 Wiggin and Dana, LLP (2001). Effective relationships with franchisee associations – Legal and practical aspects. *ABA Forum on Franchising*. https://www.wiggin.com/wp-content/uploads/2019/09/effective-relationships-with-franchisee-associations.pdf
6 Sparks, J. (2010). Quiznos settlement among largest in franchise history. *Blue Mau Mau*. https://www.bluemaumau.org/story/2010/08/16/quiznos-settlement-finalized-among-highest-penalties-franchise-history

Chapter 10

Franchise Trends

Thus far, we have described how to qualify a business for franchising, and how to build, develop and support a franchise system. We also have explained how to successfully perform franchise relationship management, which is important for maintaining equilibrium and harmony between a franchisor and its franchisees. Each of these components must be properly executed to achieve success as a franchisor. Attempting to develop a flawed franchise model, can be as disabling to franchise system development, as failing to monitor and support their franchisees.

Since the rise and development of the franchise industry that began in the 1950s, there have been several significant trends and events that have impacted the franchise industry.

The Franchise Rule

In the 1950s and 1960s, as franchising was experiencing significant growth the popularity of franchising resulted in significant franchise fraud and abuse which led certain states to enact franchise relationship laws designed to prevent franchisee abuses. These actions by certain states led to the Federal Trade Commission enacting The Franchise Rule in 1979 which set forth various regulations that franchisors must follow when selling franchises including the use of the Franchise Disclosure Document (FDD). These regulations continue to govern the offer and sale of franchises.

The Great Recession

Another occurrence that impacted franchising was the Great Recession of 2007–2009 which became the longest recession since the Great Depression. Accounting firm PwC reported that after years of steady growth the franchise industry lost 400,000 jobs in 2009. This was a significant economic event which upset the ongoing growth of the franchise industry and represented a unique economic impact on franchising. The Great Depression

DOI: 10.4324/9781003034285-10

led to poorly operated and marginally attractive franchise brands to drop out of franchising. Franchisors implemented more sophisticated franchisee recruiting strategies including targeting more qualified franchise prospects which could lower the risk of franchisee failures.

In this chapter, we discuss how current trends in franchising will lead to future changes to key components of the franchise business model. These changes defined below include technological innovations including Artificial Intelligence (AI), Digital Technology, and Robotics. Also, we discuss how the use of AI will provide more effective franchisee recruitment processes. We will present examples of how the use of AI, Robotics, and Digital technology in residential services, home care, and food franchises is being deployed by franchisors to increase productivity and the quality of products and services.

Our discussion involves more efficient ways to audit and support franchisee performance that will continue to evolve as franchisors seek ways to improve their methods for retrieving KPIs and to quickly identify top franchise performers along with those franchisees who require support. Technology will enable franchisor staff to retrieve franchise data and conduct virtual franchise site visits more easily. Finally, the structures and future role of private equity (PE) firms continue to occupy an increased role in the franchise industry. This affects franchisor expansion strategies, operational plans, and franchise owner exit strategies. PE can create more powerful franchise systems which can enable franchisors to grow and operate more efficiently with ample investment capital and business intelligence.

The Role of Technology in Franchise System Development and Operations

Franchisors are increasingly turning to the use of technology to improve their operational elements. At the franchisor level, technology is being used to automate franchisee recruitment and development tasks. At the franchisee level, automation has been applied to simplify and enhance the customer experience and increase franchise employee productivity.

The technology that's being introduced by franchisors consists of:

- Artificial Intelligence (AI) is the use of computer systems to execute tasks that typically require human intelligence such as visual reading, speech recognition, decision-making, and language transformation.
- Robotics is the use of robots (machines) to perform tasks that are performed by human beings.
- Digital transformation is the practice of using digital technologies to design or convert current operational processes and consumer practices to meet changing business and market needs.

These technological applications have been introduced and utilized in a number of elements in the franchise business model.

Franchise Development and Technology

Although a successful franchise system is built on a foundation of franchise training, support, marketing, and positive franchise relations; franchisors from the beginning of their franchise operation pursue franchise development as a top priority. Franchisee development represents the process franchisors utilize to attract, qualify, and transact future franchisees. As the franchise industry continues to expand into more business concepts, recruiting qualified franchisee candidates for system development has become intensely competitive. Although a successful franchise program can assist in the franchise recruitment process it is essential that franchisors utilize the appropriate tools to attract, qualify and engage the franchise candidates they seek.

As franchising has evolved over the past several years there have been several significant changes in the franchise development process driven by the increased use of software and technology. For example, adapting and infusing technology into franchising has eliminated countless manual processes including intaking prospect data to respond to their questions. As a result, recording relevant prospect information manually, like sorting out which franchise prospects are interested in a particular market or territory has been eliminated. Software is being used to sort franchise prospects into various categories based upon specific personal characteristics including occupation, financial profile, and location. This can enable franchisors and franchise brokers to reach out to those prospects who most closely match the franchisee profile. More accurate and intensive franchisee prospect screening software utilized by third parties provides franchisors another tool for increasing the precision when qualifying franchise candidates.

Jeff Lefler, founder and CEO of franchise market research firm, Franchise Grade explains that a recent concept in franchise development is an online one-stop portal for people seeking a franchise opportunity. To attract the attention of potential franchisees, franchisors will need to recruit prospects in more ways than just advertising in trade magazines or relying on franchisee referrals like in the past. Rather, franchisors need to ensure their online presence is optimized, with influencers and testimonials that can help get them in front of the right franchise candidates.

A one-stop franchise portal consists of a single prospect entry point, where prospective franchisees can explore and compare their potential investment. Artificial Intelligent (AI) –powered algorithms can make recommendations and help with the matchmaking process, based on the person's specific needs, objectives, skills, and abilities. Once the person is matched to a specific franchise opportunity and indicates their interest, this system can communicate to the franchisor and cue the engagement process. This technology eliminates the need for prospective franchisees to jump from one website to another to find the information they need because it would be in one central place. Lefler states that a growing variety of technological solutions is found in almost every corner of an evolving franchise system and embracing this technology will help to increase franchise brand profitability and competitiveness. Franchisors will still need to have influencers, which are reviews and testimonials touting their franchise, websites able to display the data on computers as well as mobile devices, updated social media, and live streaming.

As franchisors continue to embrace the use of technology in its franchise development programs, they will utilize predictive analysis for franchise system investments. This includes objective performance data and benchmarking against other competitive franchise opportunities. Franchisee candidates with access to objective franchise performance data will minimize franchisee investment risk. In addition, this information would enable franchisors to learn how they compare with other franchise investment opportunities and where improvement is needed. Franchisors need to embark on this paradigm shift because additional data is needed to support franchise system growth.[1]

Franchise Operations and Technology

Technology has been introduced into various components of franchise operations by numerous franchisors. From residential services to fast food to homecare, more and more franchisors are looking to technology to increase franchisee productivity and enhance the customer experience. An example of the future role of technology in franchising is exemplified by franchisor, Neighborly, based in Waco, Texas, the parent company of 27 home service brands and more than 4,300 franchises in 9 countries and 8 corporate support centers. Mike Bidwell, president and CEO of Neighborly states that they are pursuing predictive analytics, which is the use of data, statistical algorithms, and machine learning techniques to identify the likelihood of future outcomes. This can be a tool to optimize opportunities to enhance their franchisees' growth.

In the food category, Tracy Skeans, COO of YUM Brands, the mega franchisor which operates Habit Burger Grill, KFC, Pizza Hut, and Taco Bell, stated that the restaurant job of the future will require strong people skills and the ability to leverage technology and be digitally savvy. Skeans said Yum increased its investments in technological tools to make the restaurant jobs easier and more fulfilling. The future of the restaurant is going to be younger employees who've grown up in a digitally native way, no one is going to sit and look at a binder to be trained anymore.[2]

BrightStar Care one of the leading home care franchises uses a proprietary technology called the Athena Business System (ABS). It includes time and attendance of caregivers, who use a mobile device to clock in and out. The franchise operator gets an alert if the caregiver is late which enables the franchisee to let the client know their caregiver is on their way or send another caregiver. Also, when patient assessments are done, the system will instantly generate an electronic plan of care so clients, family members, and nurses can view it. Finally, the system generates five questions for each visit. If any of the questions are answered affirmatively regarding a patient's condition the agency's nurse is automatically notified. It creates management by exception that helps to prioritize a nurse's time by responding to the most needy client immediately.

Another increased use of technology in franchising is evidenced by McDonald's which acquired Apprente, a 2-year-old startup in 2019. Apprente specializes in voice-based conversational technology. After that transaction, McDonald's entered a strategic relationship with IBM to build AI-powered customer care solutions and voice recognition applications. IBM was reported to be acquiring MCD Tech Labs to further accelerate the development of AI automated order taking.[3]

Franchisors can employ technology to help grow their franchisee business. Reis & Ivry's Frozen Yogurt Robot is a fully automated franchise that uses machines to serve the yogurt. The franchisee can lower employee turnover and reduce certain expenses that come with owning a yogurt shop. The machines can be installed in high-traffic areas across the country, from shopping malls to college campuses, without having to lease a store front to place them in. Robotics is also being used in several industries. Large quick-serve restaurant franchisors continue to introduce and test robots who can flip hamburgers and perform other labor-intensive tasks.

Various forms of technology can benefit franchisor expansion because it can mean less work for franchisee employees. This can enable a franchisee to buy and operate multiple franchise units. Also, by operating more efficiently, franchisees can free up valuable time, so they can focus on managing additional business' locations.

Franchisee Performance Evaluation and Support in the Future

When a new franchisee launches their business, they are responsible for the operation and performance of their franchise. However, in most franchise systems the franchisee also relies upon their franchisor for periodic evaluations of their franchise performance and the delivery of support services. The role of technology especially AI, Digitalization and

Robotics will continue to play an increased role in franchise development and operations. As this trend continues it will alter how franchisors currently measure individual and collective franchisee performance and support their franchisees.

As technology continues to play a greater role in franchisee performance evaluations and support services, franchisors should be cognizant of these impending changes and adapt their operations accordingly. This can enable franchisors to effectively compete by demonstrating to franchise prospects that their franchise operates on the forefront of technology.

Keith Gerson, President of Franchise Operations for FranConnect, a leader in franchise management performance systems states that enhanced franchise data increases visibility and supports formal franchisor performance plans for franchisees. He states that one of the biggest differentiators among franchisors will be the use of software that increases visibility across the franchisor's span of control and allows for detailed analysis of franchise performance, both individually and as a network. These solutions will aggregate all the key performance metrics into a single, easy-to-digest dashboard. Utilizing this intelligence Gerson sees the introduction of what he refers to as the "Franchise Success Coach (FSC)." This person would access KPIs, to monitor their franchisees, develop action plans and track progress. To achieve this objective, the franchisor will need to evolve its hiring, training, and ongoing development of these "FSCs" into true performance coaches and mentors.

According to a comprehensive 2021 study conducted by Franchise Business Review, the top drivers of franchise performance (based on input from 28,056 franchisees) consisted of 5 categories, marketing and promotional programs, innovation and creativity, effective use of technology, system-wide communication, and training and support programs.[4] Gerson states that the delivery of the five key drivers will be dependent on franchisees' engagement and execution. The goal for franchisors is to find ways for franchisees to perform better and with fewer obstacles. The knowledge gained through this research can then be applied during coaching sessions with franchisees.

Although franchise brands have various approaches to franchise business planning, the most successful franchises brands are leveraging technology to establish structured programs that utilize both data and coaching to achieve desired results. As previously stated in this chapter, AI and Machine learning are finding their way into franchising, particularly in operations management. In the future, many brands will elect to keep their coaching virtual and those in the food sectors such as quick-serve and sit-down restaurants will hire food safety auditors to visit franchise locations in person.

The Future Role of PE in Franchising

Since 2010, PE firms have played an increasing role in the franchise industry. PE firms have noticed the attractive appeal of investing in franchise systems due to the unique features of the franchise business model. Successful franchise systems are highly scalable with dedicated franchisees who have a financial stake in the franchise system and work hard to provide a steady income stream. These features allow PE firms to bring capital and management expertise to certain franchise brands to facilitate their growth and earnings potential. The majority of PE firms desire investing in larger franchise brands however some firms will invest in franchises with a minimum of 75–100 locations. Many PEs invest in back-office support, marketing, franchise development, new market entry, product development, and technology and raise supply chain efficiencies.

As the first author, I authored an article in 2018 that reported on the increased activity by PE firms and the recent acquisition of the 3,600 Sonic Drive-In fast-food chain by Inspire Brands which owned Arby's and Buffalo Wild Wings. At the time it was reported that Sonic had been facing intense competition from fast-food giants, McDonald's, Burger King, and Wendy's. Three years later the role of PE groups in acquiring and investing in franchise brands is expected to increase even more.[5]

PE's role in the franchise industry includes food franchises, homecare, fitness, residential services, and automotive services. For example, in 2019 there was more than $450 billion invested in six hundred healthcare-related PE deals. In the last 10 years, the number of PE-based deals has increased by 45%, which has increased the valuation of certain home care companies by increasing operational efficiencies and investing financially in more resources.[6]

According to Bain & Company, a PE goal is to achieve a return on investment that beats the stock market which typically sees annual returns of 5%–10% depending on various sources. The returns are slowing down, but the broad category it dubs "consumer" still returns 1.5–2 times equity and beats the market by low single digits.[7] PE firms' investments range from a single franchise brand to investing in multi-unit franchise brands.

Recently, more PE groups have turned their focus to investing in franchisee-owned companies that own multiple franchise brands or multi franchises of the same brand. For example, in 2020 FRANdata reported that Bandon Holdings, one of the biggest franchisees in the Anytime Fitness system, received a majority investment from PE firm Fireman Capital Partners to help fuel its growth. In addition, one of the largest Pizza Hut franchisees was acquired for $190 million by Olympus Partners.

Due to the increased PE investment in franchising, there remains the possibility that a PE firm can have a negative impact on a franchise brand. As a PE firm invests in a franchise with the goal of generating a financial return within a certain period of time, it could encourage an increase in franchisor system growth. This could result in the franchisor signing borderline unqualified franchisees and encourage existing franchisees to invest in another franchise despite lacking the required capital or management skills to operate multiple franchises.

Alicia Miller, a former franchisee and current Managing Director of Catalyst Insight Group, which advises PE groups and franchisors, states that PE investors continue to gain influence, if there is a need, PE will improve the systems they acquire, adding experienced managers and improving unit-level profitability When investing in similar franchise systems there are cost efficiencies through reductions in corporate staff and outsourcing key functions such as call center support. As PE firms need to eventually sell the business upstream to another investor or take the company public, achieving growth targets within a period of 3–8 years is paramount.

Miller believes that certain franchise founders unwilling to invest in infrastructure or push for fast franchise development may be attractive to a PE firm that can use their expertise and capital to address these shortcomings. PE typically uses high leverage when acquiring the target (paid by the target, not the PE firm). We will thus see more debt-laden, PE-backed franchise brands, earlier in their lifecycles. High valuations also force PE to move more aggressively to justify those valuations by pushing harder for growth. Brands that are unable to find a PE partner or find a PE-owned platform in their market segment before their competitors, will find it much harder to grow and attract capital. This may force the vast middle brands to address the issues that have been handicapping the brands' growth and success.

Current PE activity in franchising indicates that it will continue to play an increased role in the franchise industry in the years ahead. This can provide an opportunity for qualified franchise systems seeking to accelerate growth and earnings and cause more franchisors to seek to sell their franchise equity for a fair price.

The Pandemic of 2020–2021

The Pandemic of 2020–2021, considered one of the most impactful events in the past 100 years, has had significant impact on the franchise industry. Franchise research firm FRANdata reported that 10,875 franchises closed permanently. The closures were led by the Hospitality, Restaurant, and Retail food sectors, followed by Personal Services, and Commercial and Residential Services. Unlike independently operated businesses, royalties and continuing fees which are built into the franchise financial model enabled franchisors to provide financial relief to its franchisees by suspending, reducing, or forgiving those fees. This enabled the survival of countless franchisees despite the impact from the Pandemic. Each of these events had a significant impact on franchising to varying degrees. Currently, there are trends taking place within and external to franchising that will have a future impact on franchising.

The recent Pandemic led certain franchise sectors to seek ways to overcome its impact. For specific franchise categories such as fitness and gyms, the solution was to implement virtual workout sessions for members. For other franchises, it meant accelerating planned changes to minimize the loss of customers and lower operating costs.

Franchise hotel brands accelerated the use of robots to deliver items ordered through room service to a guest's door. A boutique hotel near Apple's headquarters has a robot butler that can move between floors to take items such as toothbrushes, chargers, and snacks to guests. These digital systems make it easy for hotel staff to deliver items to guests, as well as offer a futuristic digital experience to people who stay at the hotel. More franchise hotel chains are using technology including online check-in and check-/out, mobile keys, and cloud-connected keyless hotel locks.

In the franchise food categories, which account for 45% of franchise industry revenues, franchises such as Chick-fil-A closed indoor access to its restaurant but added faster customer drive-thru ordering plus pickup and delivery services. No franchise sector has felt more impact and implemented more changes because of the Pandemic than food franchises. There is little doubt that franchising and especially food franchises will continue to undergo change as they evolve in the years ahead.

John Gordon, of Pacific Management Consulting Group, specializes in the restaurant industry. Gordon states that an important consideration going forward for food is the actual size and location mix of the franchisee location. This is particularly true with restaurants, which, even with delivery and carryout, serve guests in a concentric circle around their locations. Gordon adds that the leading global restaurants have begun to modify their store profile, opting for service windows, more drive-thrus, curbside pick-up, and more customer access, while downsizing traditional dining room seating.

There have been trends in franchising that have led to permanent changes in the franchise industry. These changes range from how the franchise industry is regulated to the introduction of technology in the franchise business model. Certain changes may be transitory while others will have a long-lasting impact on franchising.

Summary

In this concluding chapter, we presented current trends in franchising and how these trends will evolve and change the franchise industry in the years ahead. The introduction and use of technology by franchisors have started to transform franchise development, franchisee performance evaluations, and franchise oversight and support. Also, we explained how these changes, supported by newly introduced technologies will enhance the customer experience and increase franchise employee productivity. We discussed how the increased role of PE investment in the franchise industry will lead to more consolidation among certain franchise brands and empower other franchise to grow larger. Finally, we presented the impact on franchising brought about by the Pandemic of 2020–2021 and the changes made by franchisors that enabled franchise brands to survive.

Notes

1 Teixeira, E. (2017). *Using Applied Technology to Improve Franchise Development.* https://www.franchising.com/articles/using_applied_technology_to_improve_franchise_development.html
2 Rugless'R (2021). Restaurant worker of the future. *Nations Restaurant News.* https://www.nrn.com/technology/restaurant-worker-future-needs-heightened-digital-and-people-skills-expert-says
3 Tangermann, V. (2021). McDonalds partners with IBM to replace drive-thru employees with AI. *Yesterday.* https://futurism.com/the-byte/mcdonalds-ibm-replace-drive-thru-employees
4 May, 2021. The top drivers of franchise performance. *Franchise Business Review.* https://tour.franchisebusinessreview.com/posts/the-top-5-drivers-of-franchise-performance-new-research/
5 Teixeira, E. (2018). Franchise fast food continues consolidation as fast food chain sonic is acquired. *Forbes.* https://www.forbes.com/sites/edteixeira/2018/09/26/franchise-fast-food-industry-continues-consolidation-as-sonic-drive-in-chain-is-acquired/?sh=6ed57fd3481d
6 Nelson, B. (2020). Home care and private equity: Examining investment and quality of care. *Axxess.* https://www.axxess.com/blog/financial/home-care-and-private-equity-examining-investment-and-quality-of-care/
7 For private equity, growth is everything. (2019). *Franchise Times.* https://www.franchisetimes.com/franchise_finance/for-private-equity-partners-growth-is-everything/article_491ab1bd-5866-5aaf-b55f-394e9b8d5337.html

Index

Page numbers in *Italic* refer to figures; and in **Bold** refer to tables.

Printed in the United States
by Baker & Taylor Publisher Services